❧ I Have My Own Song for It

Akron Series in Poetry

I Have My Own Song for It
MODERN POEMS OF OHIO

EDITED BY ELTON GLASER
& WILLIAM GREENWAY

THE UNIVERSITY OF AKRON PRESS

AKRON, OHIO

The University of Akron Press gratefully acknowledges the Ohio Bicentennial
Commission for its generous Legacy Grant in support of the publication and
distribution of this book.

All inquiries and permission requests should be addressed to the Publisher,
The University of Akron Press, 374B Bierce Library, Akron, Ohio 44325—1703.

First edition 2002

05   04   03   02   5   4   3   2   1

LIBRARY OF CONGRESS CATALOGING-IN-PUBLICATION DATA

I have my own song for it : modern poems of Ohio / edited by
Elton Glaser and William Greenway.

   p.   cm.—(Akron series in poetry)

Includes index.

   ISBN 1-884836-81-x (hardcover : alk. paper)—ISBN 1-884836-82-8
(pbk. : alk. paper)

   1. American poetry—Ohio.   2. American poetry—20th century.
3. Ohio—Poetry.   I. Glaser, Elton.   II. Greenway, William,
1947-   .   III. Series.

PS571.O3 I3 2003

811'.50932771—dc21

                          2001007092

To Betty and Helen

Contents

🦋 Down Country Roads

⋙ Through Small Towns

✎ In the Cities

Preface

Anyone opening this anthology may have, at the beginning, some questions about the book: Why now? Why these two editors? And why these poems?

The first of these questions is the easiest to answer. In 2003, Ohio celebrates its bicentennial, a natural occasion for a summing up of the state's history and achievements. While Ohio can proudly point to its material accomplishments in such areas as agriculture and manufacturing, it can also take pride in its rich literary heritage, both as the cradle of writers like Sherwood Anderson and Hart Crane and as the inspiration for works like the poems in this anthology.

Not since early in the last century has a book like this one appeared. In 1911, Clement Luther Martzolff edited *Poems on Ohio,* a collection of verse more notable for its affectionate feelings about the state than for its lasting value as poetry. It is time now for a more modern vision of Ohio, a gathering of poems whose language is fresh and resonant, with a perspective that may be personal or historical, close-up or wide-ranging, in contemporary attitudes towards the character of the state.

Why is this anthology edited by two poets who are not natives of Ohio? That circumstance is partly a matter of accident and opportunity. When the Ohio Bicentennial Commission organized its Literary Advisory Council, both of us were invited to serve as members. And as Elton Glaser was, at that time, director of The University of Akron Press, he was in a position to propose that an anthology like this be published in the Akron Series in Poetry. Further, between the two of us, we have lived for forty-five years in Ohio, long enough to understand what our adopted state means to its residents. As poets, too, we have the experience to appraise poems for their aesthetic qualities. Outsiders by birth, insiders by poetic training and practice, we bring to the anthology a dual perspective that informs and balances the book.

Being born in Ohio, or even residing here, was not a criterion for either the editors or the poets whose work was chosen for the book. And neither was literary reputation. This is not a collection of Ohio poets, famous or otherwise, but a volume of poems about Ohio. In fact, some prominent native poets, such as David Wagoner, Kenneth Koch, and Richard Howard, are not represented here, because they have written little or nothing about the state. Well-known Ohio poets like James Wright, Mary Oliver, and Rita Dove—all of them Pulitzer Prize winners for poetry—are included in the anthology, but so are poets, native or not, whose names will be new to many readers. Although some poets who appear in the book still live in the state, others may have done no more than pass through Ohio on their way to someplace else.

The emphasis, then, is on the poems, not on the poets. We had only two criteria for inclusion (though perhaps we were not, in a few instances, strict constructionists of our own laws). First, the poem must be in some way recognizably about Ohio. Second, the poem must be aesthetically successful, with interesting language, compelling imagery and figures of speech, and an incisive form shaped to its subject. Some of the poems we considered worked well as poems but seemed to be more generically about the Midwest, with no identifiable Ohio features. Other poems were overtly about Ohio, often in a mode of buckeye boosterism, but lacked the depth, authority, and polish we required. Altogether, we read more than 960 poems, either submitted to us or sought out in books, and from that number chose the 117 poems in this anthology.

The organization of the book was suggested by the poems themselves, which fell into affinitive groupings that seemed preferable to the default position of alphabetical order. What eventually emerged from our sorting of the works was a kind of virtual tour of the state, from the natural to the urban, as the poems settled around lakes and rivers, farms and open country, small towns and large cities. A final category was left open for those poems that did not directly have geography as their focus, that were more inclusive or various in their concerns, or that concentrated on material we could not easily fit into any of the other divisions.

Some of the poems, of course, could be moved comfortably to other sections of the book, as subjects often overlap. And while most of the poems are about specific places, it should be said that they are just as much about people, reminding us of John Keats's remark that "Scenery is fine—but human nature is finer." Ohio is more than an outline on the map; the state comprises its inhabitants as well as its topography. Love, death, marriage, birth, friendship, family—these subjects are as distinctive and familiar as the streams and pastures, the main streets and industries that characterize the anthology.

Finally, this book would not have been possible without the support of many people. The Literary Advisory Council gave our project its impetus and approval from the beginning. And the anthology is a true collaboration between two of Ohio's finer institutions of learning, The University of Akron and Youngstown State University. We are grateful to The University of Akron Press for nurturing our project and bringing it to publication. And we thank those members of the Youngstown State University community whose help allowed the anthology to be completed: Reid Schmutz and the YSU Foundation for its generous grant and the individual contributors to the publication fund, Thomas Atwood, Ronald Baldine, Jennifer Bosveld, Dr. Bege Bowers, Dr. Steven Brown, Dr. Albert Celec, Lori Dailey, Dr. Janice Elias, Dr. Philip Ginnetti, Lynette Host, Maxine Houck, Jim Lepore, Dr. James C. Morrison, Dr. Kong and Mrs. Gim Oh, Juliene Osborne-Knight, Dr. Paul Peterson, Chester Rufh, Susan Russo, Jill Schmutz, Terry and Cynthia Sheban, Dr. and Mrs. Thomas Shipka, Mary B. Smith, Timothy Smith, Dr. Stephen and Marilyn Sniderman, and Dr. Sandra and Capt. C. Alan Stephan; Dr. Thomas Shipka, chair of the Department of Philosophy and Religious Studies; Dr. Barbara Brothers, dean of the College of Arts and Sciences; and Youngstown State University, which also awarded William Greenway a research professorship to edit the anthology. And we owe a debt of gratitude to all those poets without whose work there would be no book, no sustaining vision of the people and places that make Ohio what it was and what it is, two hundred years after its birth as a state.

James Wright
Beautiful Ohio

Those old Winnebago men
Knew what they were singing.
All summer long and all alone,
I had found a way
To sit on a railroad tie
Above the sewer main.
It spilled a shining waterfall out of a pipe
Somebody had gouged through the slanted earth.
Sixteen thousand and five hundred more or less people
In Martins Ferry, my home, my native country,
Quickened the river
With the speed of light.
And the light caught there
The solid speed of their lives
In the instant of that waterfall.
I know what we call it
Most of the time.
But I have my own song for it,
And sometimes, even today,
I call it beauty.

Along the Waters

Ann E. Michael

River by River

As we drive through Ohio,
my son names rivers
we must cross:
the St. Joseph, the Tiffin,
the Bad. He seeks
for blue lines that move
without graph-paper
regularity
as they intersect
the interstate.

Maumee. Toussaint,
which he can't pronounce
because, he says,
it looks French. Portage.
His finger moves
eastward along the route
to the Sandusky and
the Huron, the Vermillion
and the Black. "You know,"
he says, "there's a lot
of rivers here
I never noticed."

And it is true—
the road rolls over them.
Over their serpentine paths,
a straightaway
hedged with barriers
almost manages
to make rivers
inconsequential:

green-edged, brown-bodied
waterways glimpsed
briefly at 65 miles an hour,
no more important
than the ubiquitous
K-Mart or Sunoco station.

So many times I've
traveled this road
with its rivers familiar as
porch rails or doorknobs:
after the Rocky, the Cuyahoga,
the Mahoning. Highway
at noon adopts a
watery sheen, a course
navigable only by illusion;
we ply our way across Ohio—
river by river.

Diane Kendig

Lake Hope in Early Spring

Three-tenths of a mile straight down,
a red-faced goose swims in this lake,
this green horseshoe rung around
the hill where we camp, a warm-blooded pair,
our third fingers still vibrating
with their quoits. We see no other mammal,
though we arrived in a heat wave
that should have wakened us all.
Like medieval pilgrims
who looked and shouted *mon joi,*
we two kings of the journey laid claim
to the view. Startled Appalachia lit up
in yellows, greens, creams—all lost in snows
that followed. Now, sharp williwaws play
through the grounds, singing: by day, like a man
stroking a saw, wah-wah, or benign ghosts,
in barbershop croons, then keens;
by night, like snares left on during a flute solo.
They rattle the trash bags fringing the barrel lids.

We see birds everywhere: the goose, the hawk
scrawling its spirals, a crow
faking hawkhood till it flaps too soon
and caws, the vesper sparrow
with its chestnut shoulders, shouldering
the wind, and a woodpecker, rattling the silence, too.

Nothing can rattle us. We heap fire at the weather,
read, hike, and shout joy at the vista.
We're coupled and coupling, two live ringers
as long as our vision holds out, the hill
holds up, this lake holds on.

Crossing Mac-O-Chee Creek

There's always another side
to an issue or a creek.
It's getting there that's difficult.
We saw the fallen trunk that stretched
almost across, not quite.
Brambles had piled up at the edge,
with leaves and dried moss
where we tilted like cranes
wing-testing for takeoff,
or squatted like toads to regain
our balance. Farther along
you snapped a dead branch,
kicking it loose into sudden water
grabbing it away downstream.
For awhile we forgot where we were,
concentrating only on one wedged foot
after another, the next
precarious handhold of air,
debris from high water that sank
at a touch. Then, mind and body focused,
sudden as our decision to cross,
we claimed the farther bank.

Rita Dove

The Gorge

I

Little Cuyahoga's done up left town.
No one saw it leaving.
No one saw it leaving

Though it left a twig or two,
And a snaky line of rotting
Fish, a dead man's shoes,

Gnats, scarred pocket-
Books, a rusted garden nozzle,
Rats and crows. April

In bone and marrow. Soaked
With sugary dogwood, the gorge floats
In the season's morass,

Remembering its walnut, its hickory,
Its oak, its elm,
Its sassafras. Ah,

II

April's arthritic magnitude!
Little Joe ran away
From the swollen man

On the porch, ran across
The muck to the railroad track.
Lost his penny and sat

Right down by the rail,
There where his father
Couldn't see him crying.

That's why the express
Stayed on the track.
That's why a man

On a porch shouted out
Because his son forgot
His glass of iced water. That's

Why they carried little Joe
Home and why his toe
Ain't never coming back. Oh

III
This town reeks mercy.
This gorge leaves a trail
Of anecdotes,

The poor man's history.

Wingfoot Lake

(Independence Day, 1964)

On her 36th birthday, Thomas had shown her
her first swimming pool. It had been
his favorite color, exactly—just
so much of it, the swimmers' white arms jutting
into the chevrons of high society.
She had rolled up her window
and told him to drive on, fast.

Now this *act of mercy:* four daughters
dragging her to their husbands' company picnic,
white families on one side and them
on the other, unpacking the same
squeeze bottles of Heinz, the same
waxy beef patties and Salem potato chip bags.
So he was dead for the first time
on Fourth of July—ten years ago

had been harder, waiting for something to happen,
and ten years before that, the girls
like young horses eyeing the track.
Last August she stood alone for hours
in front of the T.V. set
as a crow's wing moved slowly through
the white streets of government.
That brave swimming

scared her, like Joanna saying
Mother, we're Afro-Americans now!
What did she know about Africa?
Were there lakes like this one
with a rowboat pushed under the pier?
Or Thomas' Great Mississippi

with its sullen silks? (There was
the Nile but the Nile belonged

to God.) Where she came from
was the past, 12 miles into town
where nobody had locked their back door,
and Goodyear hadn't begun to dream of a park
under the company symbol, a white foot
sprouting two small wings.

Fast Opera

It was as if no instrument other than a dulcimer
could play in the hills of that river valley,
and several of my friends began to teach themselves

to play. Nothing else fit as perfectly on the lap
or in the hands of so many who came to Marietta
from other places, a city where the Muskingum
and the Ohio crossed each other in a *T.*
This city had hosted travelers for many years,
filled its brick streets with small bars to quench

myriad desires. But sound is primal, and that valley
demanded a noise that would roll and float,
pushing like a fast opera that sets toes tapping,

crashing into the world like barges on the rivers
coming from Weirton or Pittsburgh. Summertime:
dulcimer arias had to compete with cicadas

and paddle boats, the calls of children free
for a few months. But on early winter mornings,
when only birds, small animals, and serious

farmers are truly awake, each flitting over
the thin snow, I would lean out my window
to see if the creek had frozen or still ran.

Motionless and focused on weeping willows,
I could hear dulcimer music, melodies plucked
from hay and hills, notes gliding into the ground

as the barges plodded to bigger places,
as squirrels found nuts, as my friends joined
the past and Marietta got lost in the rest of the world.

Daniel Johnson

Twentieth-Century Cave Painting, Circa 1975

The Cuyahoga is still burning
on Ohio's limestone walls.
Under a sky of factory smoke,
the river burns blue, orange, and green.

A man is lobbing his line into the water,
a red Folgers can beside him.
The charcoal figure turns his face
from the heat. A barge
plows past shaking flames.

The man's bobber is black.
His pole arcing. He hefts a largemouth
out of the fire. Holds the striped fish
close to his beard, wriggling
the sharp barb loose. It's not clear

whether the man is tossing the fish
back into its burning house. Or about
to let the fish flop and flop on the dusty bank
for centuries. A helicopter hovers.
A candy bracelet of cars is stopped

on the bridge. The fisherman
grips his catch by the lip.
Its big mouth full of wind, its tail
jerking water. The river's skin
is burning. The man's
bait can is full.

Ed Ochester

Selling Books at the James Wright Festival in Martins Ferry, Ohio

The very name of America often makes me sick, and yet Ralph Neal
was an American. The country is enough to drive you crazy.
        —James Wright, "The Flying Eagles of Troop 62"

The sign said WRIGHT FESTIVAL but
the street was closed, and a hundred kids,
little ones, were shouting and crawling
around the cracked macadam, and a long-haired guy
with a bullhorn was yelling at them and
another sign said HOT WHEELS and I said
"Jesus, how are we going to get to it?"
and Britt said "we'll have to carry
the books five blocks," but later

inside, drinking coffee, Annie said
"if James were here he wouldn't be inside,
he'd be out there with the children,"
and during the long afternoon, even after
the children had vanished, I kept thinking
how little I've ever understood, resigned
to that impatient stupidity imprinted
in our gene pool since my ancestors stumbled
around in the East Prussian mud, and it wasn't

until the dinner catered by Henry Lash,
who has the baggiest pants I've ever seen
and who hitches rides with his utensils and food
and said "I've never *not* got a ride," or until
a few beers at Dutch Henry's with the local
prom queens and the man with the plastic shoes
who was seriously peeing on the john wall
and said "evenin'" or until I saw how happy
Elton was about going home to New Orleans

and heard him tell how his daddy bought crabs
and shrimp and crawfish for a boil because he
was happy too; not till then, or later, at night,
did I understand what Wright loved here,
these strange flowers of lives growing
above the oil-slicked shore, just as
in the thirties in Europe people sang
and danced and made love and I remembered
the photo of a couple raising their hands

as if in victory, in Madrid, just before
the Civil War broke out, and I thought
as I drove over the high humpbacked bridge
into Wheeling past the Marsh-Wheeling Cigar
sign how during the early forties despite
rationing my parents held as often
as before their poor feasts and they
were lovely as the necklace of lights
yellow and white on the river that runs

through America, bloated and polluted,
imperturbably to the Gulf.

Ruth L. Schwartz

The Swan at Edgewater Park

Isn't one of your prissy richpeoples' swans
Wouldn't be at home on some pristine pond
Chooses the whole stinking shoreline, candy wrappers, condoms
     in its tidal fringe
Prefers to curve its muscular, slightly grubby neck
     into the body of a Great Lake,
Swilling whatever it is swans swill,
Chardonnay of algae with bouquet of crud,
While Clevelanders walk by saying Look
     at that big duck!
Beauty isn't the point here; of course
     the swan is beautiful,
But not like Lorie at 16, when
Everything was possible—no
More like Lorie at 27
Smoking away her days off in her dirty kitchen,
Her kid with asthma watching TV,
The boyfriend who doesn't know yet she's gonna
Leave him, washing his car out back—and
He's a runty little guy, and drinks too much, and
It's not his kid anyway, but he loves her, he
Really does, he loves them both—
That's the kind of swan this is.

Ruth L. Schwartz

September, Edgewater Park

We've come here to read about love
carved in stone—
Tammy - n- Jimmy 4-ever,
Howard loves Suzy, 1990—
      and then the tiny, wildly tufted
caterpillar, nosing briefly
through these etchings of devotion,
onto the mortal skin of your palm,
crawls back to the sweet cracks
between the lovers' names.
Over our heads, most of the trees
a ceiling of unbroken green—
and yet a few already stippled,
tipped with red and gold,
the way our softest skin, near forty,
creases us, the way the water folds
over and under and over itself,
onto the stony shore.
Once, past darkness, on this beach
I watched a man playing accordion,
rocking the battered instrument
over his big belly, lungs of song
shutting and opening—
and how he fingered forth the notes
through all the years of losses in his hands.
The taste of fall is in us now,
the crispness of the apple,
final promises of corn—
and every night, the way the sunset
burns and burns
along the length of us,

the way we burn, so fiercely,
every time we love.
Sometimes, when the waves coast in,
they don't know where they've been.
Sometimes they seem a little puzzled
as they break, with all the gladness
of water, against the rock.
Still they go on rolling, tender, shining
like the newly born.

Hale Chatfield

In Ohio: The Names of Rivers

At least twice each day
I cross the East Branch
of the Cuyahoga River
(etc.—

the geographies of duty,
routine details of topology);

I brush my teeth; no
romance in that (though
if they had Indian names
I could sail them off like otters
across the river of this poem);

America's a catalogue
to anybody flipping through;
living in it's
something else—
more like a job or marriage:
a thing familiar and tedious
and full of a kind of love which
isn't fireworks so much as
heat and work;

I brush my teeth
in any case, and the water's
good: the feeling of having done
what's necessary and
moving on.

Dorothy with Richard

Dorothy likes poems that remind her of when she was fourteen and stood on a hill overlooking the Ohio River and promised God and herself she would be happy even if one of them had to compromise, that being happy was the least a person could do to show her appreciation.

She was Deedee then, Dorothy says to Richard in Richard's bed.

Deedee dreaming of Dorothy lotus-legged on a Sunday morning, the window up, the sun and its churches of birds coming right in—which is how Dorothy speaks to Richard, his head on her lap while she peels them two oranges, because this is the poem he wants.

≈ *Ron Domen*

Beaver Creek

*the voice of the turtle
is heard in our land.*
—Song of Solomon 2:12 (KJV)

There was a time when flowers
had thoughts and the hills heard
turtles speak of the brilliant colors
of things growing and butterfly
festivals and cricket fantasies
of red hepaticas and windblown
asters on sultry summer afternoons.
When fog lingered in late morning
light instead of escaping to Post's
Woods or Trotter's Swamp along
Little Beaver Creek you stopped
by the empty barn and sheds
at the end of an alley forsaken
and mournful as the coal mines
and coke ovens that surrounded
your small Ohio town.
You painted the hard buildings
and splendid trees with heavy strokes
of raw sienna and ocher
yellow and black never failing to show
*the strange white light that hovered
around the edges.*

*(Inspired by the journals and paintings of the
American painter, Charles Burchfield [1893–1967])*

the barges at night on the ohio river

are invisible, though there's some sense of presence
in the unlit quarter mile between the blinking yellow
bow light and the white light at the stern of the tug,
something more than just that heavy throb of twin diesels
pushing the high-riding, empty string upstream.

the river grows a little darker as they pass, a tow
five barges long and three across, slow against
the current, seen, for awhile, from the kentucky side,
backlit against the downtown cincinnati glitter,
like some gigantic spaceship crossing the starry sky,

a blankness in the plenisphere at first, black hole
that could suck an errant vessel in that never saw it,
shred some innocent pleasure boater stem to stern
and spit him back while the tug's small crew went about
their evening business, drinking coffee, watching the VCR,

and the captain flicked his searchlight over the shoreline,
picking out the green marker right where he knew it was.
it's happened. it'll happen again. it could happen
to you, cruising at night away from your dock or
out of some small tributary, the great, dark, unlit mass

of the river ahead, your head filled with the whine
of your own I/Os, the last thing you ever hear or know
before you find yourself inside the high-walled canyon
of the barges. they're on their way upriver, after coal.
maybe at wheeling a deckhand'll find something splintered,

wedged between two barges, not a tree this once. maybe
he'll even know what it is, maybe recall some momentary
shudder in last night's passage, while he was dealing out
a hand of euchre, as if an engine skipped one heartbeat
and he saw the next day's work laid out for him. maybe not.

Puberty

Remember the way we bore our bodies to the pond
like raccoons with food to wash? Onto the blue,
smooth foil of the gift-wrapped water I slid

my embarrassing self. All the water I knew
was from books. I had read of the surfless Adriatic
and read how the North Atlantic erected by night

its wavering cliffs of fog and cul-de-sacs of ice,
only to turn to the dawn its chill, placid cheek.
But twitch and thrash in my chair as I might,

it was true what the swimming teacher told me:
once you learn how to float, it's almost impossible
to go under. I tried and tried, and so I can tell you

how we greet the news by which we survive: with rage.
A bucolic boy adrift on a Xenia, Ohio, pond?
Not on your life. Like you, I gulped and learned to swim.

Ray McNiece

The Stretch of River between Belpre and Marietta

Never since the chemical plants
and refineries raised their shining bodies
to begin seething, shift after shift,
has the river in these stretches
my old man told of
spoken its own name.

Oh, it wanted to, many summers
as it limped by doomed elms that pulled it up
and spread it leaf-taut.
Along some sloughs corn still stands still,
sheening and June-full.

At the confluence with the Muskingum,
there are men with farmer's tans—
the kind where your throat, biceps, and neck
are burning, and the rest of your skin is untouched—
there are men wading and fishing with doughballs
for channel cats that plow down
and down, eating, cleaning,
remembering the current's curves.

On their way to work at the plant,
they don't have time to lament much
of what passes.
My cousin who has worked there for years
gets nosebleeds sometimes for no reason.
For no real reason, the preacher says,
the kids around here
are blowing their minds out.

When the river bends around
around by Belpre,
even under the cover of darkness,
it will not utter a single vowel or ripple
of its origins and changes
because there it is—
cylindrical, illuminated, steaming, manifested—
the plant stands and hums.
And the river there moves like a rat snake
through a sewer pipe.

On a day the sun was doing everything it could
to make the water appear half-healthy,
on a bluff above Marietta, the sulfur upwind,
we watched as you spoke for yourself, for us,
for all the good it would do,
you said, Ohio, and again,
muddling along, Ohio.

Ron Antonucci

Final Nature Poem on the
Little Cuyahoga

This river smells like wet dog.
A cardinal dips
blood-bright above the water's yellow
rush over slime-slick rocks.
A jammed fishing reel hangs tangled
from the dusty brush on the banks.
A slack blue bag droops. An oil quart.
Brown filter tips clutch together, smoked
and soggy.
Two beer cans: one, flattened, glints in the mud;
the other, suck hole up, bobs in the eddy.
On the shore, a flourish of fast food Styrofoam
like torn flowers, in colors that never match.
A swallow, belly feathers matted and combed
by last night's rain, lies eyeless in the muck,
danced on by fleas and flies.
And me:
my neoprene sole stirs up
clear backwater pools,
making a monster foot
no Iroquois ever had vision of.

Anniversary Poem

A young couple drowned last summer
on Lake Erie, in the calm water
we could see from our honeymoon
window. For us a year's gone by like nothing,
but the future out in front of us, light and buoyant,
no longer seems certain as a destination.

Married just a year, their destination
was peace and quiet, a cabin and a summer
week alone. They rented a boat, the clear water
of the lake suggesting a second honeymoon
unmoored from everyday concerns. Nothing
weighing them down—the clouds buoyant

as spinnakers above them, their hearts buoyant—
they kissed their way to a new destination.
Time did not stop, but sailed faster. One summer
hour melted into three, him buoying her up in the water.
(We didn't get our feet wet on our honeymoon.
Friends asked us what we had seen. Nothing!

Each other!) When they looked up again, nothing
could be seen of the boat. Guideless and buoyant,
it had drifted away, seeking its own destination.
They had forgotten to anchor. Some mere
oversight. The husband swam for shore. What were
her choices? She swam after him, the honeymoon

over. (Meanwhile, we stayed in bed, honeymoon
sex a destination reached over and over, nothing
to slow us, our bodies rising together, buoyant,
first one on top, then the other, destination:

pleasure, as much as we could squeeze into one summer
afternoon.) They swam until they took on water,

until their arms and legs turned to water,
then weighted and sank. For three days, I mooned
in front of the television set, watched nothing
but the local station. The unnervingly buoyant
reporter said *presumed drowned* like *destination
of choice.* A double anniversary this summer:

our honeymoon, their deaths. Sun-swelled, buoyant,
the summer days slip past us like bubbles underwater.
We're nothing if not destined to drift on.

Home in Ohio

How difficult to say anything
simply, to utter
I am happy.

I am. This street
a wonder of sunlight
and leaves, the cats so present
in their grace.

The kids play base-hit with
a red beach ball. One
twelve-year-old cartwheels
home, blonde hair fanning
like light off a saint.

The tallest trees never heard
the word *achievement,* and beyond the hill
the muddy slow river arrives

and arrives.

Down Country Roads

Anthony Libby

Lost in Ohio

Small roads in Ohio go nowhere,
they wander searching, as if thirsty
for an ocean they've never seen,
only felt in the traces of salt
on the feet of far-wandering travelers.
Dying for water, sometimes they swallow
an unwary farmer walking at evening
to the 7-Eleven. But more often they hover
peacefully around farm ponds
and man-made lakes slick with the tanning lotion
of country girls, smelling of coconuts
that never were. And the roads
accept their lot, somewhere beneath them
the ghosts of failed rivers,
dune dry, and making the best of it.

Judy Klare

Homesick

Here the vast silent fields wait;
spring is late,
or perhaps will not be at all—
windmills idle since fall
look even less enthusiastic now;
no small stir of daffodil
or fountains of forsythia spill
into this western April.

Azaleas?
Rhododendron?
Not here. Winter is overrun.
And I said goodbye
to dogwood this year,
the surprise of magnolia in the air,
a redbud's staccato note,
early flowering crab and pear,
or the green drift of tulip trees
on one impatient Ohio hill.

Snow is gone
but winter's last-minute marathon
crawls slowly toward June.
Fields near this town wear brown.
A few birds, though,
seem to be in tune:
one file of robins is crossing the lawn
in perfect formation,
finches ride the pussywillows,
juncos and cardinals nose to nose
work the garden.
And squirrels, too,
more ardent than I,
greet this faithless sky.

The Family Farm

Two generations out of mind, the family farm
almost calls out from chasms the strip mines
left like open maws among the hardwoods,
almost shouts hay, corn, pumpkins, rocks,
almost lures us with its blackberry vines
back to southeast Ohio where the wide porch
grins like a possum.
                    But even my father,
now past seventy, remembers little of that old
sweat and bother, the long, humid summers
burning with flies, the outhouse wild with wasps,
winters bone cold and gray, and the brick school
too close to get away from.
                  His father sold out
to a total stranger and moved to town,
leaving the family farm like a forgettable dream
to haunt him when the lumberyard went down
with the good ship Lollipop.
               Now we almost
think of going back, full speed reverse
past the turn of the century when a bushel of corn
almost brought a fair price and children grew up
oak slow, gentle among milk cows mostly
black and white.
             But no, this is just a visit,
Cousin Hilda, we can't stay. We're just checking out
the old homestead, got to wondering about
the pumpkins and whether you can make it
on just hay and blackberries, or whether the rocks
take over no matter what.

🐝 *Robert Bly*

Driving through Ohio

I

We slept that night in Delaware, Ohio:
A magnificent and sleepy country,
Oak country, sheep country, sod country.
We slept in a huge white tourist home
With *National Geographics* on the table.

II

North of Columbus there is a sort of torpid joy:
The slow and muddy river,
The white barns leaning into the ground,
Cottonwoods with their trunks painted white,
And houses with small observatories on top,
As if Ohio were the widow's coast, looking over
The dangerous Atlantic.

III

Now we drive north past the white cemeteries
So rich in the morning air!
All morning I have felt the sense of death;
I am full of love, and love this torpid land.
Some day I will go back, and inhabit again
The sleepy ground where Harding was born.

Deanna Pickard

Not Poor

Cicadas are squeaking like loose wheels
on a buggy even he can hear. He tells
of their mating weeks that must last
for seventeen years. And another summer
story of locusts, when farm wives

battled with useless aprons
while the corn turned to widow's lace
and their men were hard pressed
not to fold. The children, too, knew
nights would come to whiskeyed words,

as mothers blinked back the beaten
silences. Another truck would carry them
to another place. Thoughts of no gifts,
not even hardtack or used shoes next winter,
would hover overhead like buzzards

but since lightning bugs were torching
the trees, the heaviness in the house
would allow them to sneak out to collect
the free jewelry of those Ohio nights.

Kevin Prufer

Two Muses Discuss Arrowheads

Two sloop-shouldered thin-legged young men beneath the Texaco sign
in Ohio, off state route 62, in the late afternoon, wearing blue jeans,
eating grapes:
      Find them all-the-time, the first one says, splitting the green skin
between his thumb and index finger. *Got them sharp points, got them sides
cut through your hand*

      *if you hold it too tight. Look like leaves, look like
no stone I seen around here. Shine in the sun, flinty, knob-ended, sharp,
sharp as busted up bits of skeet.*
      The clear juice of grapes
trickles down his fingers, into the dirt. He holds up his hand. *Big as my hand,*
he says, *but longer, thinner.* His hand is beautiful, smooth and pale.

His hand has that glow of a car's headlamp coning the white mist in a dark road.
It is perfect, glistening, juice-slick. It seems to say, *watch me, watch me, watch me—
I could sever myself,*

      skim the field-furrows, dig myself beneath the corn.
Around his feet, a scattering of discarded skins of white grapes, some dust-covered,
some pure and shimmering in the going sun

      and the young man holds his hand up
a moment longer, flexes his long fingers into a point, *like that. Got me
a boxful.* His friend carves a long arc in the dirt

      with his white shoe, shifts
where he sits on the curb's edge, nods, agrees. The sun goes down. The bright sign
glares. Like a thousand edgy little thoughts, the other thinks,

the arrowheads glow in their quiet places beneath the empty cornfields.

In Ohio

White mares lashed to the sulky carriages
Trot softly
Around the dismantled fairgrounds
Near Buckeye Lake.

The sandstone blocks of a wellspring
Cool dark green moss.

The sun floats down, a small golden lemon dissolves
In the water.
I dream, as I lean over the edge, of a crawdad's mouth.

The cellars of haunted houses are like ancient cities,
Fallen behind a big heap of apples.

A widow on a front porch puckers her lips
And whispers.

The Sumac in Ohio

Toward the end of May, the air in Southern Ohio is filling with fragrances, and I am a long way from home. A great place lies open in the earth there in Martins Ferry near the river, and to this day I don't know how it came to be. Maybe the old fathers of my town, their white hair lost long since into the coal smoke and the snow, gathered in their hundreds along the hither side of the B&O railroad track, presented whatever blades and bull tongues they could spare, and tore the earth open. Or maybe the gully appeared there on its own, long before the white-haired fathers came, and the Ohio changed its direction, and the glacier went away.

But now toward the end of May, the sumac trees on the slopes of the gully are opening their brindle buds, and suddenly, right before my eyes, the tough leaf branches turn a bewildering scarlet just at the place where they join the bough. You can strip the long leaves away already, but the leaf branch is more thoroughly rooted into the tree than the trunk itself is into the ground.

Before June begins, the sap and coal smoke and soot from Wheeling steel, wafted down the Ohio by some curious gentleness in the Appalachians, will gather all over the trunk. The skin will turn aside hatchets and knife blades. You cannot even carve a girl's name on the sumac. It is viciously determined to live and die alone, and you can go straight to hell.

Ohio Farm House, ca. 1846

The glass-blue days are those
when every color glows,
each shape and shadow shows.
 —G. M. Hopkins

At least six cats called; dogs barked by every tree;
    iguanas, goats, lizards in a cage,
        spavined horse, then the pot-bellied pig

sniffed our shoes as we hung
    from the pasture fence,
        and the parakeet flew

room to room, our accompaniment
    in the blue house. The smell rose
        from plaster walls, from the dirt basement

where bees simmered in a nest, from the dark hole
    of the kitchen sink, from the mudroom.
        It's that pee smell, the realtor said,

but she was wrong. The rich manure tea
    the farmer spread across the garden
        each spring wormed its way

beneath the fence, across the gravel yard,
    cataloguing, as it went,
        the molecules of age, decay,

the care and relief of the farmer who sat
    twenty feet away from that creeping
        spore-casting cloud beneath ground.

He carried a pole chair to the porch
        and rocked on those four legs.
                It's a still-life from above, or from

the receding point as we drive away.
        But beneath, it burns,
                and in a sun-sweat of garden earth

tomatoes writhe in their bath of steam,
        on multifoliate vines,
                and blossom.

Now the pig roots among them,
        his hocks sinking into earth;
                now he smells his own rude smell.

Losing Grace

> Yesterday, we drove into the country.
> Too green—those country roads,
trailers perched against small hillsides,
> anything old and metal tumbling down
into deep gullies, rust seeping brown into
> small, quick-running streams.

> In New Baltimore, the young waitress
> looked hard into my eyes, asked twice
if I wanted the Special—
> turkey and mashed potatoes.
> No trouble, she said kindly—no trouble at all.

> Yesterday, we drove down
> country roads more green,
> more beautiful than the week before
> —old barns falling into themselves,
> gray houses rotting behind clambering vines.

I don't know when it happens, exactly.
> The road grows suddenly strange,
> the sky too big, the fields all broken up
> and parceled out, neat little houses
> and people smiling in their yards like props
on a movie set. I don't trust any of it.
> Like trying to pick up a stitch
that's fallen, grandma would say
on one of her blue days,
> during one of her spells. We have fancy
> words for it now—this bewildered picking
at clothes or hair, mind gone blank, leaping

at landscapes, trying to latch on
to words, to a face, trying to make anything mean.

I'm giving up. I'm in no mood to hold up
this face any longer—these sad, crescent-
moon eyes. Like those tumbled down
barns, limestone splintered beneath
thick green vines, I shattered
years ago—blown into the white light
of a late Ohio summer afternoon—
that merciless white light
the world finds so benign.

David Baker

Dixie

Now if you want to drive 'way sorrow,
Come and hear dis song to-morrow.
            —Daniel Decatur Emmett
for Bob Cantwell

I

I had no idea.
In Ohio, in a field
near where we've found ourselves
blackhearted and alone,
where the winter-blanched
stalks of corn stubble stand around,
wind rasping through

their ripped sleeves, where
yesterday the whole field seemed
a sad, gray blur
after last week's scum of snow,
the Snowden brothers' twin stones
crumbled and are gone.
Proud relatives, you guessed,

or some high-minded public
servant, must have remembered
the two sons of slaves
just long enough to engrave
and raise one more
store-bought stone, there
in the backwoods churchyard

where we marched
over the grave-soft earth.
Weak light fell
through the frames of black branches

where no song was.
Only: *They Taught Dixie*
To Dan Emmett.

2
Braced by snow, but booted hard,
the back door for days locked
tight with ice gave way.
And so help us both, we tramped into
no good single story again, your home.
The logs we lugged in,
the weeping logs we stacked and lit

could barely thaw each other out
to burn. The walls glowed
with their other life, your daughters'
drawings plastered everywhere:
dazzling suns, ruby trees, birds colored
every possibility, summer pictures
like sweet outflung windows

the cruel wind blew into,
frameless as mirrors, back-looking, devastating,
beautiful. Our guitars loved us
the little they could,
two freezing singers whose lives
slept safely somewhere else
in the concurrent dark,

whose songs were stolen.
Isn't that the irony
of misplacement, that we remember ourselves
through others? The whiskey's smolder
faded late and slow. Outside
the sleet crept scraping
among the haggard trees, like a spy.

3

Uncle Dan in blackface,
Uncle Dan in greatcoat and boots stomping
across the stage-planks, deliberate
in his dirge, a walk-around so pure
with longing and regrets
the audience shuts up and stares:
In Dixie's Land where I was born

Early on one frosty morn,
Look a-way . . . upstate New York, 1859.
It's snowing, how many hundreds
of miles from Ohio
where the Snowden brothers pluck banjos
and sing for passing coaches
from their porch. He's on his way

to being famous, his minstrels
in demand, though today his white ears
crack in ferocious cold. He turns,
spanks and twists his floured hands
high in the air, though
his back seems broken
it's so bent, and now shuffles

to the other side, face colored
into a negative of clown,
singing of mistakes . . . *Look a-way,*
Dixie's Land. Camera powder explodes
and clapping scares a flock
of pigeons from their oak. He watches them
scatter, recollect, fly away.

4

Snow falls over Ohio.
I have a window so wide

it's like I'm sitting outside, easy chair
kicked back, half-drunk, freezing.
The truth is, I've been trying to write
a love poem all this time
and don't know how. She's gone

and won't come back, next-door neighbor
to your daughters in that fenced-off,
foreign country inside this one.
If I sight them right, along
my thumb, the stumps align
like crumbled, nameless, blackened stones
in a graveyard—but you know that

already. The trees
crowd around gray in their daguerreotype.
It should be spring but snow keeps coming.
There should be flowers
but the stubble field and fencerows
grow only murderous with crows.
Like little pieces

of a poem gone wrong, and torn,
the snow keeps floating down,
and she is gone.
Uncle Dan lived a long time
and I have his words on good authority:
I wish I had never writ
That God-damn song.

5
How do you tell people
you love them in this cold
country too big for its own good?
So help me, I can't stop

from seeing the children, blood-wild
and eager, trooping across
their families' fields,

the stolen song of another country
gone wrong on their lips.
I can't stop from seeing
the Snowdens starving for a song.
I had no idea
it would turn out like this.
Like some silly, lovely-painted clown,

a bluejay fiddles away right now
in the redbud's heart,
harping on and on outside
my picture window. I look away.
You would say he's full of life, old friend,
and you'd be right. You would say,
in all your hope and sadnesses,

he signals the going-on of things.
And you'd be right again, I'm almost afraid
to think. I see you sitting
in your summer-frozen house, alone,
thumbing a book, breathing into your hands,
and wish the same old wish, that we were
anywhere but here.

Hart Crane

Sunday Morning Apples

To William Sommer

The leaves will fall again sometime and fill
The fleece of nature with those purposes
That are your rich and faithful strength of line.

But now there are challenges to spring
In that ripe nude with head
      reared
Into a realm of swords, her purple shadow
Bursting on the winter of the world
From whiteness that cries defiance to the snow.

A boy runs with a dog before the sun, straddling
Spontaneities that form their independent orbits,
Their own perennials of light
In the valley where you live
      (called Brandywine).

I have seen the apples there that toss you secrets,—
Beloved apples of seasonable madness
That feed your inquiries with aerial wine.

Put them again beside a pitcher with a knife,
And poise them full and ready for explosion—
The apples, Bill, the apples!

Terry Blackhawk

Good Friday at the Rookery
(somewhere west of Akron)

In memoriam, Alan Huber Lloyd, artist and composer,
b. Cincinnati, Ohio 1942— d. New York City, 1986

Through the intervening scrim
     of last year's leaves and vines,
their nests seem like mistletoe,
     or clouds, and the traffic's din
mutes their flight to pantomime.

If only I could hear them. If only I could
     assert some selective silence.
I want the geese to stop their territorial
     announcements and the peepers
cease their high-pitched calls

so that I may listen in on the dance
     of the herons' mating. I want to cross
the fence and step deeper into the swamp
     until the traffic on this two-lane road
fades away. May the dying out of engines

be the last dying. No more vans of visitors
     or Harleys revving slowly
through the dry spring air. Just these birds'
     balancing acts on platforms
in the unleafed sycamores. I want to hear

the flutter of the male as he lands feet first
     as if stretched by some string along
the vertical. I want the click of twig on beak
     as she accepts his single stick
after each departure and return.

No more cries from noisier creatures.
No more bleats from the beasts
of Kosovo tethered in their burning stalls.
I want to understand only this:
how he plummets to the swamp floor,

then hoists his crook-necked glide into
ever-widening rings, how when he
mounts her, his wings exalt the air.
Only this, until the egg is ready
to burst its shell. Then I will sketch

these birds the way Alan did who died
over a dozen Easters gone.
I will use his unerring lines to show
how the female's crown
feathers above the thorns of the nest.

With luck I will conjure
some mad trompe-l'oeil
to fool eye *and* ear and let me hear
his vanished music.
Then I will invite them all back in—

the loudmouthed geese, ululating frogs,
folks treading gravel alongside
the road—I will bring them all in to inhabit
my wavery lines and his ink-
dark pools, the space of his unframed page.

John N. Miller

The Amish Farmer's Daughter

for Bill Nichols

It's dark, and it's winter
with no electric lighting. I can't really
see her, but I'm told
that she has left the farmhouse
and has taken an old pair of skates
down to the pond.
                    The only light
is what the ice has just absorbed,
glinting it back toward pinpoint stars.
She should be warmly bonneted,
a long, dark woolen skirt around her calves,
not knowing, as she straps her skates on,
the figure she might cut against the snow—

a distant ancestress in Rheinland-Pfalz
who trudged across subzero farmland,
bent into the cold to steal some pleasure,
skimming on wooden blades her home state's
broadest river where it seemed
frozen over at its slow shallows.

Here in midwinter-chilled Ohio
it's probably as dark as on the Rhine
centuries ago. I've never seen her
mittened hands clasped behind her back
as she bisects the pond's perimeter,
serene and stately, smooth, each measured stroke
conserving as much virgin energy
as the surface freeze allows. Now she is
racing, soaring, whirling, sometimes
falling on her well-fleshed *popo,*

squealing, shrieking with laughter, letting it
all out, until she flops down
panting on a snowbank and dumps
ice shards from her boots.

How old is she? No one has said,
and it's too dark to tell. I know she's skating—
at home on an Amish farmer's spread of ice
sufficient to sustain her weight,
large enough to exercise her skills.

The Curse of Purslane

My neighbor says if only I grew
sheep or pigs, they'd gobble up
this greedy weed with shiny leaves
that crawls all over rich dirt where
my squash, tomatoes, peppers, need
more room to spread their roots.

I hack with hoe, yank with black
fingers, pile up the rubbery plants while
my helpful neighbor says they'll only
grow back stronger, since the flowers
keep on living afterwards to ripen
seeds and plant themselves again.

Then she tells me how New Zealand
women make a tasty soup of younger
leaves than mine. Too bad I waited
until they toughed me out. I ask Ohio,
why me and purslane together in a garden?
Something to cope with, I suppose.
Like a neighbor who knows everything.

≈ Mary Oliver

The Black Walnut Tree

My mother and I debate:
we could sell
the black walnut tree
to the lumberman,
and pay off the mortgage.
Likely some storm anyway
will churn down its dark boughs,
smashing the house. We talk
slowly, two women trying
in a difficult time to be wise.
Roots in the cellar drains,
I say, and she replies
that the leaves are getting heavier
every year, and the fruit
harder to gather away.
But something brighter than money
moves in our blood—an edge
sharp and quick as a trowel
that wants us to dig and sow.
So we talk, but we don't do
anything. That night I dream
of my fathers out of Bohemia
filling the blue fields
of fresh and generous Ohio
with leaves and vines and orchards.
What my mother and I both know
is that we'd crawl with shame
in the emptiness we'd made
in our own and our fathers' backyard.
So the black walnut tree

swings through another year
of sun and leaping winds,
of leaves and bounding fruit,
and, month after month, the whip-
crack of the mortgage.

Mary Oliver

Stark County Holidays

Our mother's kingdom does not fall,
But like her old piano wanders
Slowly and finally out of tune.
There are so many things to do
She rarely plays it anymore,
But there were years of Bach and Strauss;
The chords flew black and rich and round
With meaning through our windy house.
We fell asleep, we wove our dreams
In that good wilderness of sound.

At Christmas, when we all come home,
The table's stretched with boards and laid
With linen; in a festive ring
We sit like heroes trading tales.
But lately in a little while,
Among the talk of art, or war,
A kind of hesitation comes;
A silence echoes everything.

Afterward we rise and file
Behind our mother to the fire.
With stiffened hands she thumps away
In honor of the holy day;
Hymns and carols rise and hold
As best they can on blasted scales.
We listen, staring at the night
Where faith and failure sound their drums,
And snow is drifting mile on mile.

Our mother's kingdom does not fall,
But year by year the promise fades;
Dreams of our childhood warp and pall,
Caught in the dark fit of the world.
Now, less than what we meant to be,
We watch the night and feed the fire.
We listen as the bent chords climb
Toward alleluias rich but wrong;
We sing, and grieve for what we are
Compared with the intended song.

Taraxacum Officinale

Early spring, the first light
still vague, nacreous, glacial
and nothing of the season in the air
but rain, the gray and lateral
sweep of limbs above the roof
a scrawl, a line drawn in spindle and spine—
nothing of the season in the mire
of wasteplace and field
but the wildflower the French call *dent-de-lion*
for the serrated edges
of its basal leaves.

In this light, this moment,
this might be home, my mother
alive again, in love with the turning
of the year, down on her knees
in the fields of the Ohio Valley
to harvest the greens: alchemy of earth, wind,
and water, a sort of sunlight
on the tongue,
the walk home somnolent, her work at the sink slow,
the kitchen tamped down,
doorway and window.

The rain falls, now incremental,
measurable across the vertical
light, the endless pattern already begun
in the parry of root and knife,
then the leaves in a moment
darken to bitterness, and the blowball, blowzy

on the wind, relays desire
or fidelity promised,
and what remains in the hand—tally of lapsed
time—is counted, seed
by seed, hour by hour.

Glenn McKee

Summer of 1912

Three sisters with faults
no bigger than being born
in a mountain shadow,

hung around all summer
like coats on a hall tree,

waiting for a man
who'd wear them out
with work and childbirth.

Ellen Renée Seusy

The Compost Bin

All winter, and in all seasons,
I feed this dirt from my own kitchen,
taking the long walk into a deep yard.

Out of the yellow light of the house,
stepping down from the din of appliances,
out of rooms stuffy with television,

I sink into a pool of light on the snow
and pause to balance two bowls
heavy with limp celery and red cabbage.

At the edge of the light, I look down,
then step out into Ohio's dark night,
into what used to be forest.

The yard is quiet. This cold walk through the dark
takes me far, and who knows what will bloom
from what I bring? At the wooden bin

I tip the bowls onto the snowed-over compost.
Chemistry is going on in there
that I don't understand, and bright peonies

could come from this decay. Sometimes
I wish not to go back, but to stay out
by the soft-armed hemlocks,

out here by the compost bin,
this hearth way in the back of the yard,
and deep inside, the fire that no one lit.

Steve Brightman

Benefits of Geauga County

I fell asleep before the 11:00 news
and stayed on the couch
until the dog woke me up
at 2:30 A.M.

I took the eight groggy steps
to the sliding glass
door and realized
I had to go, too.

If I were living in Lyndhurst
or Columbus or Massillon,
it never would have entered
my mind.

But I don't live in Lyndhurst
or Columbus or Massillon.
I live where I can hear
the seasons change.

Where the dog and I
can go outside, side by side,
and strain to hear fall
creeping up on summer.

Suckering Tobacco
(Miami County, Ohio)

Heat-stroke sun;
    only Hank and I
    left to sucker all this tobacco
    back by the cool green woods
    where I ride fallen trees
        like wild stallions.

Tall stalks of tobacco
    hide my long colt legs.
    Hank Taylor's eyes
    hotter than sun's
    dart across sweating
    tobacco rows
    to my belly,
    brown between shorts and midriff.
        I pull at them, hide my navel.

Hank's eyes dance from me
    to the woods.
    I pull suckers from ripe tobacco
    before they flower—
        sow wild seeds.

Hank edges closer.
    Pulls fat worms
    from their hiding places.
    Says there's wild strawberries
    bigger than his thumb
        just waiting there in those woods.

Wet hair sticks to my neck.
   I say we didn't bring anything
   to put them in.
   Hank says we'll eat them.
   I say we've got to sucker
   this tobacco before sunset.
         Hank says those suckers can wait.

Kathleen Iddings

American Beauty
(R.R. #1, Covington, Ohio)

While kerosene gushed out the spigot
    into a jerry can by the back door,
    Mother pulled jeans from a rusty line
        and hurried to stir potato soup.

Kerosene ran for an hour
    soaking the foundation of our home,
    deep into dry soil,
        down to the roots of our rosebush . . .

Climber, its glorious red that bloomed
    all summer at the corner of the house,
    survived Ohio blizzards and tornadoes,
        the only color around the gray farmhouse.

Farmhouse that stole my mother's youth
    with its eternal clotheslines
    and endless sucking oil stoves,
        demanding as nine empty bellies.

Took her youth as surely as kerosene
    strangled our rosebush.
    Don't anyone light a match! she shrieked
        when she remembered.

I wonder if secretly she wished
    it would ignite,
    flare red, bright
        and brief as the roses.

Moose Ridge Apple Wine

1

In August, on the township roads,
the blacksnakes stretch themselves
across the rocks and hard clays
so you have to stop the car.
Then they coil themselves,
lift their slim, sleek heads,
and twitch their tails like rattlers.
If you grab them,
you will find how hot the world is
in the summer,
and your hands will smell like dead meat
for three days.

2

In the roadside ditches
where the weeds twist thick,
the minor lizards—skinks and swifts—
tour the sticks and tendrils
with quick eyes. Beetles glint
like jewelry on the undersides of leaves;
deerflies choir on mouse skulls,
green cutworms slash at thin stems
with their sharp and sidewise jaws.
On a smooth stick, invisible as air,
a mantis hacks a small wasp into splinters,
holds a flash of wing in claw.

3

Sober, high-noon seeing,
these sudden sightings from the car:
these stumps, these cold springs splashing on the rocks,

these dead hawks in the mulleins
with the black and yellow beetles
big as nickels on their rotting wings.
Things to see, to make a lifetime of,
to carry home or drowse on,
to curl a dream around.

4
But daylight lasts a long time
in the summer: it is not yet time for sleeping.
And now, the old Ford hot from climbing,
the big woods break
along a saddleback of ridge,
sunlight shimmers on a gatepost,
and in the middle of a field
of thistles, joe-pyeweed, and nettles
sits Mr. Hummel's shack.
A thousand silver dollars
in the mortar of the mantel!
A cask of double eagles under floorboards!
And Mr. Hummel, confident, at ease,
sits smiling on the porch
as you pull in on the gravel.
When you unfold, sweating, from the car,
katydids whirr off in all directions,
and a house wren rides the high scale
in the buckeye by the porch.

Moose Ridge, August,
Hummel's apple wine!

5
Around here, men who have the time,
and men who make the time,
sit all day at Hummel's,

and they let their extra money leak away
like rain down Wolf Pen Creek,
then heal their empty places
with Hummel's home-made wine.
His moon-eyed hound that rocks
and hobbles on its three good legs
won't drink it,
but that means nothing to a man.
Mr. Hummel pours a saucer
on the porch steps,
but all it draws is flies.
"By God," he says, looking at us all,
"That dog is dumber than a pounded nail.
The best days that I've lived,
I've lived them wild and drunk."

6
The wine is deep in pickle crocks,
as gold as cider,
as cold as good well water.
You drink it from a dipper.
"Seems all I'd see
was pretty women in them days
when I was drinking hard stuff
on the river," Hummel says.
"Saw one, God's truth,
in Beaver Town one time
that had a head of red hair
like a bonfire. And she was warm
in other spots."

We pass the dipper all around—
me, Jim Winland, Ealy Fishbeck,
and old Hummel, already shuffling cards.
"We'll play some euchre, boys,
then get another drink,

then we'll do the block and tackle."
"Block and tackle?" someone says.
"Yessir," Hummel says.
"You drink enough of that,
you walk a block
and tackle anything in sight."

7
Hours later,
and the sparrows
roosting in the eaves.
The trump invisible, the point-card
gone with oak leaves in the breeze.
Jim Winland leans against a porch post,
Ealy Fishbeck wads a fresh chew,
loose as hay, fatter than a walnut,
and me and Mr. Hummel
pick the wood ticks off his hound.
"I've never seen no sense in ticks,
I'll tell you,"
Mr. Hummel says.
"Near everything I know
says ticks don't make
a bit of common sense.
Now even your tapeworm's
good for laughs, at least—
that cure that has a fellow
set his chin against the table
and then yawn,
and how that tapeworm
sashays out his mouth
to find that dish of milk
he set there—
but ticks!
By God,
they've beat me."

Ealy Fishbeck snorts,
and says,
"Hummel, life ain't all romance."

8
And then the moon hangs
like a ghost-fire
in the buckeye,
bats spin from the chimney,
and a big moth floats slow
above the white hood of the car.

Darkness.
Everything you've seen
by day has bought the black suit
and gone home.

Silence.
Rustlings in the weeds.
Then, a flare of light
from down the porch:
Mr. Hummel stokes his apple pipe
and somehow, as you sit there,
smoke makes all the shapes
of creekbends, blacksnakes,
of thrushy thickets
that the birdsong washes from
in rivers you can see,
and it is the best sight,
night-sight now,
the sweet wine climbing
to your eyes, and it is sleep, and all
the secret unspoiled places of your sleep
you want to float to,

down the rivers deep inside you,
slowly,
from this upland, weed-shored shack,
late at night,
in August,
in Ohio.

Ivars Balkits

Regional Bird

The wild turkey says Yes! to existence.

Flocks abound in the squatter's lower thirty or more. Seven poults and a mother. One tom gobbler, bearded, blue-cheeked, copper. They leave peace signs in the snow.

I've got to have one, not for dinner but for conversation. I have a turkey calling.

Part of the forest pulls away and lets the missile fly. The sporting weapon has three nocked at once and operates on gizmos and pulleys.

I've seen twenty or more. Thirty or more. Wild, tall-necked. I've mistaken them for storks. I've mistaken them for buzzards.

That's because I've been a city-to-city boy. An Interstate resident, I say Yes! to exits. I say, Quik Mart, call me at your convenience.

I want to rap with Ben Franklin's symbol.

Wild, and turkey, too. They had to be reintroduced to Ohio. I want to know how that's possible. I want to be reintroduced to Ohio, too. Ohio. Halloo. Appalachia. Hello.

I say Yes to your regional bird.

David Shevin

Rebecca Devanney, 1954–1981

In a boiling pot of horseflies and straw grass
and black-eyed Susans and some wild purple
burgeons, I realized it was twenty years
since I sighted you wild in a clearing

somewhat like this one, but South, and far away.
What have you done in the earth all these years
while we've only completed emotional business
in dreams or the spirit world? I was driving

down roads with dried stems for their borders.
One side of the road was a green wall of corn
and one side of the road was a green wall of beech
which stopped at a willow. When I stood

in the day's burn, the air held the feel
of wild Irish hilarity, heavy with green and the efflux
of the big insects' season, the buzz of the field.
I thought you the only flower in the dangerous world,

and too soon we learned just how dangerous.
So we know, and enough now. Enough of this death,
sleeping infant. There is too much new music
to hear, and the jerk of sleep is too short a time

in which to share all that this kind life deserves—
yes, kind despite all the ulcers and lost blood
and fortune that goes who knows where.
Check out what today has in Seneca County

upriver from the Izaak Walton League house:
heavy and pollinated air, a hot moment that grabs you
all close and stickier than a shadow, sweeter than sex,
big as all Adam and almost—almost in all the day's

cloud and the new moon's chrome—almost virgin
all over again.

Joanne Lowery

Roof, Ohio Territory

We had the smallest cabin in the settlement,
ten feet to a side. That June it rained
heavy a hundred times, our corn sodden.
At night we'd take up most of a wall
and listen to more falling. Be grateful,
I told myself, for the roof he made.
It works: I can hear each separate
beat, the only music we ever hear.
Despite the slope, some trickled in
to muddy the floor, cold snakes waiting
to find my toes. So afterward I'd stay
and wait till morning to go out back.
Early next spring, hail and wet snow
broke the center beam while I labored.
Wet hissed in the hearth with our son's
first cry, a boy who grew up rich enough
for floor and shingles.

Mary Crow

Finding Wild Bees on My Sister's Farm
near Baltimore, Ohio

The swarm of bees droops from the apple tree
in a ripe pear shape, deep brown,
an angry buzzing under the damp bough.
But, the beeman says, their bellies
are so full of honey you can pick them up
and take them home to your hive.
Hold the box for me, please.

How must it be to gather that buzzing
into its own box, closing the lid
on the deep pear of the swarm, queen
in the center and the drones
clinging in their multitude
to her homing instinct,
her sex?

The blossom-pink branch bends
from that angry weight. The moist air
lies heavy with dew and heat, spring
coming on like a bitter wreck.
My body puffy with humidity,
with jet lag, is dark with its own sting,
its own brown honey.

Stanley Plumly

Tree Ferns

They were the local Ohio palm, tropic in the heat of trains.
They could grow in anything—pitch, whole grain,
cinders, ash and rust, the dirt
dumped back of the foundry, what

the men wore home. Little willows,
they were made to be brushed back by the traffic of boxcars
the way wind will dust the shade
of the small part of a river.—They'd

go from almost green to almost gray with each long passing,
each leaf, each branch a stain
on the winded air. They were too thin
for rain—nothing could touch them.

So we'd start with pocketknives, cutting and whittling them down
from willow, palm, or any other name.
They were what they looked like. Horsewhip, whipweed.
They could lay on a fine welt if you wanted.

And on a hot, dry day, July, they could all but burn.
At a certain age you try to pull all kinds of things
out of the ground, out of the loose gravel thrown by trains.

Or break off what you can and cut it clean.

Mennonite Funeral in Southwest Ohio

for Gayle King

On this November hill, once far away,
beside women's hair capped in devotion,
we stand bare as trees and outdoor hymns.

The lives of barns roll into each other
below this churchyard where our prurient eyes
measure the widow's silent life. This morning

strong people with backhoes and history
part the merciful earth, and the dead farmer
slips away from us, from all the autumn stalks

of work and prayer gathered in the county.
The preacher unfolds the day's passion, returning us
to glory where we never know despair,

rocking in the rhythm of the Lord,
with the Father and the Son, with the Spirit
we all feel, so polite and kind that

we have no choice but to disarm death
in the minute before we say Amen Amen
and shield our eyes from the cold sun.

Outside the church basement, we pilgrims,
so polite and kind, wait to eat and drink
the mysteries old women heap upon our plates.

We never ask what old women know of life,
the ground, or us. We raise our cups,
our children, our fear, as the women pass, smiling,

cousins of cousins, sisters, aunts, always willing
to give us more, while the farmers wait for coffee,
the next planting—wait for us to leave.

Homage to the Corn

It's sweetness, light,
all our lives. 80,000 years
we've worshipped, yet
young as June it stays.
Kernels left in earth
1000 years, fresh enough
for the archaeologist's mules,
put to flame today
still pop their blossoms.
How history nourishes,
yet such staying power
promises to wear us out.
It takes 10 natural years
for the soil to come alive
again—the plot where
corn stood up and hoisted
the stars ten feet higher.
Sometimes we hear it
out of the windless July dark
as it lifts, ticks out
some growth like love;
we wake at first light
and 4 inches of 4 horizons
are gone.
            When I go,
put me in a shallow mound,
like the ruddy ones who named
this tasseled, rustling Ohio.
Place seeds on my eyes,
between lips and thighs,

in each fist crossed
above my heart. Go away
until memory calls you
back to me playing tall
against the wind that brings
its ravenous, rattling chill:
great green bladed flames.

Gwen Hart

Losing Ohio

The things that stand still will, of course,
be the first to disappear—the long lip of the curb,
the squatting bushes, the stubborn, stalled Chevy,
the frozen features of the front stoop.

You insist on running five miles a day on slippery
shit-roads with false shoulders, their ditches humped
over with snow. You run alongside traffic until the roar
of snowplows makes you jump over, lose
your legs in snow, stand in it up to your waist.

Whole convoys will pass December this way, flashing
and dragging metal, at the end of the road where the mailboxes
hibernate, their black, hungry mouths iced shut,
their bodies shaky from the slams of road-clearers.

You sleep with your good ear muffled
in a goose-down pillow while the snow settles over
the places you know well, buckling roofs,
toppling power lines, and severing telephone connections.

When I try to come back to you, the plane descending
not through sky, but through the chalky white of a snow
cloud, what will be waiting?
                                        What will I return to
if everything I've counted on is long-buried, houses
closed and hearts steeped and shuttered in snow?

Through Small Towns

James Wright

Autumn Begins in Martins Ferry, Ohio

In the Shreve High football stadium,
I think of Polacks nursing long beers in Tiltonsville,
And gray faces of Negroes in the blast furnace at Benwood,
And the ruptured night watchman of Wheeling Steel,
Dreaming of heroes.

All the proud fathers are ashamed to go home.
Their women cluck like starved pullets,
Dying for love.

Therefore,
Their sons grow suicidally beautiful
At the beginning of October,
And gallop terribly against each other's bodies.

≈ *BJ Ward*

Spring Begins in Hinckley, Ohio

For the past 41 years, the town of Hinckley, Ohio, has waited patiently for what it considers the first true indication that spring is here—the return of the buzzards. For four decades now, a flock of buzzards—also known as turkey vultures—returns each March 15 to Hinckley's rocky ledges. And this year, despite a blowing snow and sub-freezing temperatures, the buzzards did not disappoint.

—CNN 3/15/98

I

I am sure the axis of the earth
passes through Hinckley, Ohio,
because every year the buzzards drop down—
little flags of death
lowered on an ancient flagpole—
and people rejoice.
The town runs out of champagne.
How appropriate to cherish
the reinstated balance of the world—
vultures corkscrewing down as tulips squeeze
themselves open—a wrenching into tenderness—
and spring herself starts teasing out the grasses,
tuning up the wind's motor, airing out the willows' drapes,
setting up summer's bright, unlocked house.
And with life rising and eternity dropping,
Hinckley's people become suddenly and quite happily caught again
between a contralto and baritone singing the same song.

II

I am east of Hinckley—northwestern New Jersey,
where for some reason the world is still still
and warmth is a love letter on the way
via bulk rate. However, the teethed cold
outside the car can't keep this sky from blushing
as I ride partially into it, partially out of it.
Here everything outdoors is locked frozen,
but what compels me are the worms

deep beneath the ice—those puny and insistent ground vultures,
little squirming letters that spell a frightening word—
the worms who have been eating decayed
hands, buried waste, swallowing dog turds
as if they were éclairs. To have that hunger for waste—
to blindly eat the rusting rainbow taffeta
of last year's leaves. . . . I love how they love
what is used and then spoiled—how they, deep
in their wormy brains, must know that death is a factory
always in production, always in the black,
and how they set up their pantry there,
beneath the cold, immersed in the earth
where we'll all return when we are done
driving, done waitressing or practicing law,
done with grieving and done with loving
what is passing, done with eating whatever
death we eat and justify with our own vulture logic.

III
People of Hinckley celebrate one thing in two halves:
while the world opens its wide garage doors again
to thoughts of rebirth, bumper crops, and long summer kisses,
above and below us there is an ancestral motion
scribbling its uneasy language
against the sky and in the earth,
its ancient hand slowly spelling, as if in no rush,
Bring it all back through my body.

G. C. Waldrep

The Lights of Chillicothe

at 3 A.M. are no more or less
garish than elsewhere,
though somewhat less numerous.

The sign by the Quik Mart reads
"VA Facility." The arrow
points west but the lights

shine in all directions
at once, up, down, around
in their perfect halos. Southside

the Mead plant belches smoke
and the pages of this notebook
and light, tons of it,

crazy crazy efflorescence
not generally counted
among the chief exports of Ohio.

Leaving Downtown Marietta, Ohio, 1983

They leave the barges that litter the Ohio,
They leave the silos that spring up like corn,
They leave the dumps that threaten to tumble onto
The interstate from their crackling perches,
They leave the shops, the small farms, the motel lobbies.

They are downtown now as the sun
Makes a gold river from a red sky.
The stench of a hard-worked day rises
From cobblestone streets to choke our beers
And remind us what hands are for.

Free from the factory, hot off the farm,
Excused from the classroom, expelled from meetings,
Nothing matters more to us than a pitcher or two,
A game of pool or euchre,
The world cut off by willow trees and bridges.

I walked those streets all the time, the violet horizon
Of night leading me away like a star. I had surrounded
Myself with jewel-toned trailer parks and history
So bold it shimmered in the rain and on the backs
Of cockroaches. The future floated in leaves

Falling around those with glasses in their hands,
Circled the town and ran out to the Mail Pouch barns,
Then stampeded back to the downtown bars.
I saw it that night in each dim porch light,
And I finally followed it out, wringing my hands.

అ *John Streamas*

War Brides' Dinner

Who would have guessed so many women from Japan
live here in Hamilton, Ohio? Kimiko has brought
french fries for us kids and the adults have mashed potatoes
with brown gravy, which their GI husbands once ordered them
to learn to make. Still we notice—we kids sitting on the floor
or at tray-tables behind our mothers, gorging on drumsticks,
fries, and Pepsi—that it's the rice they eat completely.
Half-eaten slabs of meatloaf, pools of gravy, peas and carrots—
these remain on the plates that Fumiko and my mother gather
for washing. But no more rice. For rice is
what these women find, and what they can afford,
of foods they ate in Tokyo, Yokohama, Hiroshima,
when they were our age, before the bombs and the GIs.
For this is 1960, this is Ohio, and Kroger and IGA
carry only rice, ramen, shoyu. And welfare checks
won't stretch for fish that isn't fresh anyway.

And no, there are no men here. Our fathers are long gone.
These marriages end badly. Five years, two kids, maybe
a job driving a dump truck in Eisenhower's America,
and these farm boys, bored by Asians and restless, sulk
and maybe punch our mothers, then leave for white women
named Beverly or Ginny. No forwarding address, no alimony,
no child support. Our mothers, who've known fire bombs,
atomic bombs, Occupation, immigration, a new language,
citizenship tests, and racism, now learn loneliness.

For dessert, the women splurge on pints of Lady Borden
ice cream. One large scoop each, melting fast
on paper plates. For the first time all day our mothers,
barely fluent in English, speak in English. Kimiko raises
her camera and snaps pictures: scenes of Ohio life,
summer 1960, Asian women and their half-Asian children,
casualties of war made in occupied Japan.

Julie Herrick White

Death

I never really got to know Steubenville.
Thirteen months were not enough. We had
an apartment over my husband's parents
on Adams Street, a square brick house
near the top of the hill.

We used to slide down that hill
on cardboard boxes, my husband said.
It worked fine, as good as a sled.

Perhaps thirteen was an unlucky number.
Perhaps my homesickness was infectious,
that my husband, like me, was longing
for some other place, and in the winter
he slid away, down streets and alleys,
past churches and rows of shabby houses,
gaining speed, steering straight
for the river.

Near Liberty, Ohio

In the logged-out woods, blackberries grow up everywhere, taller than me. Surrounded by briers, a princess in her castle sleeps. All the people of the kingdom, Liberty, Ohio, sleep. Blackberries twist up at the stone walls along the interstate. Blackberries cross ruts that once were paths to milkhouses, fallen down, gone. Wake up. The princess dreams. Someone with sword on horseback will cut through. Wake up. If only the princess could get her own pretty hands on a machete or—what she really wants—a gas-powered weedeater.

Bob Cox, neighbor man, seventy-four years old, goes out back with his bush hog.

Early in spring I got up one morning to take a hoe to the trillium and the pretty mayapples with their little hearts, the insipid fruit.

Philip St. Clair

Nelson Ledges, 1948

Hiking on the rocks? Strictly for those who just don't know
>   the time: portly old maids
or gabby bachelors or the teens from the Baptist church camp
>   or the geezers who pack a
picnic lunch for Dead Man's Cave, none of them will ever go
>   into the big pavilion on a summer night,
when the smart girls in white dresses and saddle shoes
>   walk together in groups
of three or four, their cobalt-blue vials of Evening in Paris
>   hidden deep inside their purses,
giggling behind their hands at the signs above the peepshows—
>   Hollywood Scandal, What the Plumber Saw.
And the boys, hair carefully stiffened with pomade, are there
>   to stroll beside them:
they talk about music; they invoke the names of casual friends
>   and last year's high school;
they buy them dark sodas and give them the sequined kewpies
>   they have won at shooting galleries.
They feed coins to the gypsy fortune teller whose machinery
>   has been carefully sealed
in an airless booth: safe from the crowd that mills about her,
>   she swings a plaster arm
to dispense the future on a lozenge of cardboard while the moon
>   soars high above,
ignored and outdone until closing time by the thousand lights
>   that hang from side to side
over the wide boardwalk—each with a loop of unwavering fire,
>   each with a nipple of glass.

Leading Them Back

Hudsonville, Michigan,
Elkhart, Indiana, Xenia, Ohio—
In the Midwest we live with tornadoes,
those great collectors
of animals and surrealist furniture.

They pass through glass.
They choose people on golf courses,
forcing them to lie down in ravines,
their fingers gripping loose stones.

I was sleeping with my sister,
the girl said. The last thing I remember
was the radio playing, and my mother
in the kitchen. We woke up
on our mattress in the basement,
my sister on top of me.
You're taking up the whole bed,
I said. The radio was gone. My mother
had wandered off. They led her
back. Every day they led her back.
This is where you belong, they said.
These are your daughters.

And the daughters of stones
and broken dishes take their places
for the first new meal.
                                        Pass the sticks,
my sister says, and no one asks
the question of these pleasant
flat lands where the sheep
are slowly driven back,
and a new broom
                        sweeps clean.

That Summer, Joe, and Prison

I
Ohio, with its steel-toed boots,
Heels worn away on the outside.
These boots are shackled
Like a chain of Coniber traps;
Ankles, the twice-sprung necks of muskrat.
Gray day workclothes hang
From window bars by a rope.
Ohio, an inmate's sucker-punched face,
Peony face, swollen
And latticed with ants,
Its broken nose bleeding from one side.
Ohio's wrists are leashed
By leather, its puppet hands
Playing to a full house. Wooden heads
Jerking off on a day-hall rug.

Ohio then, with its petticoat sail
Skirting the lake. Bare-breasted,
Bikini top whipping a mast,
Its tin bucket full
Of bluegills dropped back.
Ohio on holiday,
Tongue licking colored ice,
A thin-wristed lover,
Sunburned and sleeping,
Its fingers, a ribboned ponytail
Twisting down the back,
Fingers that loose a rope from the pier.
Ohio, a four-pointed star
Spread out under moonlight,
Its pretty ankles
Dipping the green water.

2

Ohio, wrist under the hand of Michigan,
Riot gear stacked in hallways,
The Man figures my worth
As a hostage: young, white teacher—
Single female, with child. I'm worth too much.
He sends me home for the weekend.
Johnny Crusoe sends each pitch
Home, over the wall. Crash Redell
Glides his face through plate glass.
The Man cancels passes, fishing.
And you, slamming a ball down the alley,
Break the pinsetter's leg at the knee.

Bluegills in a tin bucket,
And the man I've invited from New York
Dangles his chicken-bone wrist
Over the side of the boat. I float on my back,
Casting into night: boathouse dinner,
Then the moon, shiver of glass,
Spreads out on the deck.

The Man called you Fat-Boy-in-Trouble, Joe,
Strapped you four ways down to a Marlowe bed,
Bread-dough belly breathing hard,
Rising naked and fast in 102 degrees,
Six-by-eight room. You called for water.
And sometime before morning,
The man from New York pissed
From the side of the boat. It was summer,
And laughing and good. The trouble, Joe,
Falling back and away from me.

Jeanne E. Clark

Tractors

Ronnie's the shortest guard in the state of Ohio
Where he is champion
And best kisser of Susan Ellen Haubner. I know.
She says my brother Ronnie kisses like he plays
Basketball, quick and hard. She says he palms her ass
One-handed. She says Ronnie moves
Between her legs as if the whole state of Indiana and its governor
Came out to see how the game is played.
Ronnie goes with a girl who can talk like that.

Ronnie calls me Einstein. I say
Umbilicus for belly button.
Bowel movement for, you know. Ronnie says,
You can't make Einstein say shit.
On the way to the game Saturday night,
The family rides in a Bel-Air station wagon,
Ronnie rides with the team. In the back of the car,
I read *Webster's Dictionary*, find
One strong word for each letter in the rival team's name:

Bungarum, venomous snake from India
Without a hood. *Ubiquitous,* existing everywhere.
Levirate, the code of Moses: the dead man's brother
Must marry the widow if there are no sons.
Languette, insect tongue. *Slocking stone,*
Rich ore luring investors into a worthless mine.

So, tonight, the Bulls will be stronger.
In the back seat of the car Ronnie will borrow
After the game, Susan Ellen Haubner will say
Basketball players have no future.
She will dump Ronnie

For Coach Jackson's son who has, as she says,
The fine, steady hands of a surgeon.

I don't know what I want. But when the crowd
Jumps to its feet, last thirty seconds,
They roar like the engines. They are all
The tractors in Ohio.

Marianna Hofer

Fall in Reily, Ohio

The maples glow with the yellow
of a carnival tent at the county fair
and drop their leaves just as the farmer's son
drops the cornsilk cigarette from his fingers,
choking behind the barn, the ground
littered with cornsilk and husks.

Three miles outside town, bark peels
from the scarred branches of the beech,
creamy white beside the barn
that kneels in the weeds, thistles banging
swollen heads against the wall
like children throwing tantrums.

Old men, their farms divided
and sold for a good price, collect
Social Security and war pensions, sit
on tilted porches in metal rockers, the paint
flaking as they rock, cordwood stacked
to the second floor window.

At night the wind gusts through town, the leaves
swirl like small bones in a whirlpool, and the old men
turn over under their blankets and keep on dreaming
in black and white.

Sue D. Burton

Brick

Don't be put off by the banal decor or the neighborhood.
—Alfred LeBlanc, in a restaurant review, The New York Times

Ginsberg had rediscovered Whitman, friend of even
the piss-ant, but Ginsberg was weird,
clinking and *oming* in an orange dress
to the undergrad premeds.
We were graduate students. *We* read Villon.
Thirty years ago and I was twenty-two. Wet-behind-the-ears-
but-no-place-else out of Ohio.
Out of a house so parched
vowels cracked when they left my mother's tongue,
my father never saying a word in my defense.
The first time I heard *banal*
was my first day of class:
a big mop-haired boy, pipe, silk cravat,
reading a poem about his father. *Banal, banal, ba-nall!*
Go f yourself!
Repeatedly. Etc.
The mortification of faking I knew what was going on,
and the icy thrill
at putting parents in their place.
Banal, I thought, was about bad art.
And my dad's lousy politics about the war.
But now—where've I been all these years?—
I see it has to do with brick.
Merci, Monsieur LeBlanc.
Like the brick in those row houses near the shipyard,
tidy two-story houses with flat shingle roofs,
nothing fancy, but not a place you'd get mugged, either,
or knifed in the back,
just a quiet everyday neighborhood
where last Friday noon

at the restaurant under review
I tasted *focaccia* to die for, Mrs. M's
homemade *tagliolini*, her *tiramisu*, ah, in a class
by itself.
But what is it about brick in *those* neighborhoods
that gives it that singed look?
Was it left in the kiln too long?
Like the face of "Uncle Reddy" Kulik who
worked the coke furnace for twenty-three years.
The same scorched brick of Republic's teetering smokestacks
and the old stagecoach road out by the graveyard
and even the new wing of the Massillon City Hospital
where I rushed back, if ten agonizing hours on a bus counts
as rushing, that year I was twenty-two
when my father had a heart attack,
where in the scrubs-green waiting room I picked up a *LIFE*
and there was a story about our town—*Typical*
Blue-Collar City Reacts to the War . . . shabby main street . . .
but at the surgical glove factory
business is booming . . . just buried the first son
lost in Viet Nam . . . a gritty block of neighbors
in their Sunday duds looking down at L.B.J.
on their Zenith TVs.
I'd never heard *blue-collar* before.
In all those years of English Lit, didn't I ever lay eyes
on a sociology text?
Two new words that year, burned in my memory,
and the image of my father flat on his back, struggling
to mouth, *You're here, Sudie.*
Memories I never thought to line up side by side.
But today it hits me like a ton of bricks.
A blue-sky'd Sunday morning, and here I am
hissing and shredding and stomping
on the *Times.*
Why has it taken me, father, so long
to defend us?

Robert Miltner

The Future of Lorain, Ohio

Low rain clouds blockade
the mouth of the Black
River where the slow
ore boats call to port.

Tumorous catfish caught
by fishermen get tossed
back in or up on the bank,
left for the river rats.

The lighthouse is an artifact,
the shipyard shut down,
the steel mill nearly idle,
Broadway vacant for blocks.

In the doorway of a boarded-
up building, huddled against
the storm, a couple presses,
making sparks in the dark.

John Knoepfle

At Marietta, Ohio

Where the Adena mounds were once,
men from Boston stockaded the bottoms,
and Putnam who mocked King George's army
led them there. They pioneered
with Indian worry, but grandsons read

the town paper to see what ships
were jamming for Asia. Welsh came after,
singing mostly through their noses,
but usually did not stay the town,
their craving still to the west for iron

farther along the valley. Germans
made a permanent coming, though,
and made the hilltops guttural;
they would not trust a river fog
dissolving Muskingum's lower farms.

Larry Smith

310 Murdock Street

(Mingo Junction, Ohio)

Long I lived in that green river valley
along the burnt edge of the mills and railroad,
knew the lights through unwashed panes
at every hour, the sounds of trains clashing
and sirens punctuating the industrial roar,
and at night the trucks shifting down
through our lives, headlights moving a pale scrim
across the ceiling cracks, voices downstairs
working things out while we children slept
through the poverty of getting by,
while the winter wind slipped under the sill
and my radio sang on the small table
before I slept, my right arm above my head
tricking the sleep on, waking to the cold
of a coal furnace, the bathroom floor a chill of linoleum,
steam rising slowly from the sink where I washed
the new day into my face, the kitchen where we ate
and talked under the dropped ceiling tile,
passing the toast to hands, emptying cereal boxes,
the television voices already selling the day
to Mother in the other room. All of us
off to school of some kind,
leaving behind the old life of closets and attic,
basement tools, our faces held in mirrors and photos,
our parents moving quiet through amber.

Drowning in Ohio

In the month of mildew, plunging thunderstorms
Crease the dark with their freak chandeliers,
Bully the roses and the loose roof.
A stink of rain
Rises from the asphalt, and the air
Bloats in a stupor of greasy swells, moping
Over the neighborhood.

Dog days with the mange . . .
Heat wraps itself around you like
A weasel on a Rhode Island Red, swelter
Even the attic fan can't suck up. The whole state
Lies down with a cool cloth on its forehead
Or moves its heavy feet in numb shoes,
Zombie with a drug habit.

Inside this downpour, the small town feels
Barbarous and raw.
You miss the spiky scent of grass, the insects'
Rhetoric by the evening porch, the moon
Looped in a cat's cradle of stars.
And the bay panes? It's like looking out a porthole
At a drenched horizon.

With any luck, a noonday sun will rout the clouds
And willows mop the mud away.
With any luck, the mercury will drop
Like a two-bit palooka, and the birds come back
To their vaudeville turns, slapstick
In the ruins of oak and pine. With any luck,
You'll find a rainbow purged of sullen promises.

Jeff Gundy

Black Cat in Byhalia

—for Sekou Sundiata

What can I say about all this, trees reaching up one at a time,
thousands and hundreds of trunks branches twigs stems
every bit in exactly its own single space, singular

and individual as the exit that I just missed in this hyperbolic
existentialist poetic trance. "Days go by in broken English"
you mutter on the tape, and oh they do. Out here they go by

without any kind of English, they just go, those trees
hold their hands up, the snow lays its easy fingers down,
everything else just flits and wobbles toward its own place,

everything has been changed by someone who isn't here now,
some set of guys who walked and tilled, plowed and planted
and strung together the power lines, phone lines, water lines,

guys who did their work and went home and left it, empty
and relentless as a cloud or the ocean a mile down.
They'll be back. Sekou, there's a lot of space here

but less room than you'd think. And there goes a huge flock,
2, 3, 400 birds moving like a stirred-up kettle,
a whirlwind of dark, small, crazy birds, splitting into parts

then whirling back together, the whole boiling mess
above one big bird, a hawk I think, all those little birds
like a black, beaked message from the God of the sharp little birds,

a sign for the hawks that out here even they had best watch
where they fly. And this is Byhalia, where the black sweet muck
grows the best white sweet Byhalia onions in the world,

where the houses seem to grow right out of the ground,
where the Evangelical Friends Church stands white and friendly
at the north end of town. And this is Mt. Victory

where I sail through a very yellow light at 33, 34 miles an hour
and nobody's coming fortunately and no police cars lurking
to drag me down and interrogate my clean white ass and so

I sail on into the countryside, past the hopelessly scenic
and defunct barns slowly crashing in like broken-down boats,
leaking those old prairie hopes of order and prosperity

and barns handed down to the children, barns that would hold
the warm dumb cows and tender sheep and hay heavy and sweet
in the loft above, barns that held the thickheaded dreams

of old men who wore themselves down getting up in the dark
to feed the stock before going to the fields, coming home
at dusk to feed the stock again, dog-tired, bone-tired,

tired to their souls and guts, and the wives waiting
with the beef roast still warm in the oven but dry, dry
and tough, and eating in the kitchen silence with the hard

overhead light bouncing on the formica table, the linoleum,
the white cupboards, nothing to say, knowing where
it was all heading, the boys gone off to the city

and the girls married to men who were drunk already every night,
men who knew only the wrong ways to use their hands.
And the barns run aground on the reefs of money and time,

the slowest and most cornily scenic shipwrecks in history,
old men dead in their dusty beds and the women dumped off
at the county homes where every morning the nurse

brings in the drugs, combs the white thin hair down over
the leathery foreheads and leaves the rest to tangle as it will.
I almost forgot, Sekou, but as I drove through Byhalia

with you asleep beside me there was this black cat, I saw it
coming on and I thought Come on, cat, you see me, you know
I'm big and heavy and you're not, but this cat just kept on coming

and I could go nowhere and do nothing but run right over this cat,
right front wheel right rear wheel just like that, boomp, boomp,
and I looked back thinking Oh, no, thinking to see flat cat

all over the road. But here's this cat in the other lane,
tail a little ragged but all its legs working it across the road,
another car just misses, this cat is annoyed and ruffled

but not even limping, I swear this cat is thinking, "Man,
how many times do I have to get run over today?" It's looking
testy and bedraggled but the cat is walking, where this cat

is heading I don't know but that is one tough black cat.

Lynn Powell

Beulah

In the Ohio of midlife, houses rest
on wide streets lush with the ordinary: phlox,
daylilies, jonquils, the evergreen, the deciduous.
Weather arrives *air mail* from the west—
breeze or mackerel sky, the evening storm
and its surrender to clarity.
The full moon drowns out a galaxy
smudged here and there. Local stars swarm.

All over town, the zeal of desire has softened.
Husband and wife sleep skin to skin,
flesh of their flesh, close to the bone.
Then, house by house, the women
stir, stumble toward tiny lamentations.
It's OK, they whisper, and the milk lets down.

Robert Fox

Walking the Streets of Portsmouth, Ohio, 1977

Six P.M.
in downtown Portsmouth
the sky blue.

In a parked Oldsmobile
a tattooed boy and his disheveled
girl stare at each other smoking.
The broken sign over the hotel
says HOT HURT.

No one watches the sparkling waterfall
in the Roy Rodgers Esplanade.
I retrace my footsteps
grin at myself in the dark windows.

The reflection of my face
becomes my father
looking out at me
I slip into an envelope of oblivion
like my parents' death.
The shards of their spirits do not remember me.
They don't even remember their own faces.
Here on Chillicothe Street
in deserted Portsmouth
I might confront
my infant son
grown to manhood
as I sometimes
found my father
in the New York subways
or outside Macy's

happy at the accidental
love that bound us.

I stand waiting
for something
a celebration
a party of festive ghosts.
My relatives could tumble
from the Chinese restaurant.
I would hold
my blood out to them
so they would know me.

The streets cool
in the blue shadows.
A country song
falls from an open window.

Baking Pies

While I climbed the sprawling green
pie apple tree, famous for its small
wormy fruit, my never-to-be-married
Great Aunt Estelle held forth in the kitchen
with her fork, cutting Crisco into the flour
and shouting over her deafness at my mother.

Didn't my Great Aunt Estelle own the best
Victorian house in Barnesville, Ohio?
Why was my fearless mother so afraid of her,
my father's favorite aunt, who could
take her teeth out with the tip of her tongue?
Her younger half-brother wore a marvelous
glass eye he said he could take out any time
and shoot like a marble, called it his taw
and said he'd take me on whenever,
but he only played for keeps.

While the pie baked, my Great Aunt Estelle,
a lousy cook, even the ubiquitous all-American
apple pie defied her, would play dominoes,
beating me incessantly, sending my tremulous
fingers dancing back to the bone-yard
among the treacherous ivory rectangles.
They were real ivory, she once said, carved
from the tusks of African elephants.
"Don't be afraid," she would say, "just play.
You can learn a lot from losing."

And that night my mother would cry
all the short ride home, my father saying
softly, it's all right, everything's okay,
a warm apple pie on her lap.

Approaching Chester, Ohio

Last night the sky ignited;
November trees blazed up
match-struck by the setting sun.
High on the hill, the old courthouse
windows flamed, then flickered
as if lit by candle glow.
Time curled back—
suddenly horses' hooves
clattered on hardened ground,
cold wheels creaked on stone.
Longing for home,
I pulled my shawl close,
(though I had no shawl or house there),
and leaned into my husband's body,
my children's breath rising behind me,
radiant, white as bone.

Basic Writing, Marion Correctional

I come each day through fields
furrowed with corn, bean and barbed wire
overseen by moonlighting farmers
perched in watchtowers, cheeks pink,
shotguns cocked to cultivate their order.
In the Visitors' Lounge the women
wait, weary from the bus ride
from Cleveland or Toledo, skirts slit
over best hose over legs new-shaven,
lips forcing smiles cold
as institutional porcelain.
In the corner a couple entwines,
his leg between hers, his hands
working beneath her blouse,
their children trying not to see.
The guard who frisks me jokes the same
each day: *You got anything in there*
but poems, Doc? I walk past The Hole
and see men come out, eyes wild
with crazy static. In the Job Readiness Room
they're all in jeans and work shirts
like my English-major classmates
at Ohio U in '69. All chain smoke
but the Muslims. They want to know
about my wife. *What color hair?*
She make you happy? You got a picture?
I tell them about comma faults.
Delivery-van doors slam gunshot-loud outside,
jerk them from their seats.
The loudspeaker thunders above my words:
C Block, Chow. Work Call: Yard Gang,

Shop Gang, Laundry Gang, Sanitation Gang.
It was coke, speed, horse
that put us here, they write, bad crowds
we ran with, bad men that hustled
our mothers, The Man who jerked us around.
I help them with their letters.
O my precious lady I ache
for the righteous mysteries of your thighs.
Dear Honey I got something I been saving up
for you. Dear Most Gracious Ladies and Gentlemen
of the Parole Board: I've changed my life.
With their pencils they want to shake
the Governor. I'm magic as a preacher,
they believe, because of words,
because each night I sleep beside a woman
and each day I've leave to touch
a son's cheeks soft as petals
of a courtyard rose rising beyond
shadows of all four walls.
They yearn to soar above cinder blocks
of each lethal year, hearts constricting
in barred cells of the breast,
hands into fists. This makes nothing
better, all admit. We're waiting
for the bell, summons from a purer world.
Time's the law, the hell men do.

David Baker

Midwest: Ode

in memoriam William Matthews

You could believe a life so plain it means
calmness in the lives of others, who come
to see it, hold it, buy it piece by piece,
as these good people easing from their van
onto the curb where the big-shoed children
of Charm, Ohio, have lined their baskets
of sweet corn, peaches, green beans, and snap-peas.
Each Saturday morning the meeting point
of many worlds is a market in Charm.

You could believe a name so innocent
it is accurate and without one blade
of irony, and green grass everywhere.
Yet, how human a pleasure the silk hairs
when the corn is peeled back, and the moist worm
curls on the point of an ear like a tongue—
how charged the desire of the children who
want to touch it, taste it, turn it over,
until it has twirled away in the dust.

There are black buggies piled high with fruit pies.
There are field things hand-wrought of applewood
and oak, and oiled at the palm of one man.
There are piecework quilts black-striped and maroon
and mute as dusk, and tatting, and snow shawls,
and cozies the colors of prize chickens—
though the corporate farm five miles away
has made its means of poultry production
faster, makes fatter hens, who need no sleep,

so machinery rumbles the nights through.
Still, it is hard to tell who lives with
more placid curiosity than these,
not only the bearded men in mud boots
and city kids tugging on a goat rope,
but really the whole strange market of Charm,
Ohio, where weekly we come, who stare
and smile at each other, to weigh the short
business end of a dollar in our hands.

David Lee Garrison

Route 4

Take it
from Dayton through corn
and soybeans to Lake Erie,
eat maple nut ice cream
from Woody's and watch
the barns drift by.
Wave to the people
lolling in porch swings
and they'll wave back.
Take your time—
stop for LIVE BAIT and fish Honey Creek,
have dinner at Bubbles Burgers,
then see a play
at the Attica Little Theatre.

Ask for directions
at a gas station and three bystanders
will help the attendant
tell you the way
to Milford Center, Marion,
Bucyrus, Chatfield, or Reedtown.
They'll all wish you a safe trip
and someone will say
Hurry back, now.
The best place to stay
is the Stay Inn,
and the best breakfast
is at the Hen House,
where you'll want to take a biscuit crust
and sop up the last of the sausage gravy.
Next door you can pick out a Bible

in purple leather for Aunt Gladys
from J & R's Gospel Gift Shop.

The welcome sign assures you that
Salvation Is All You Need
at the Mechanicsburg
Church of God,
whose fallen parishioners
lie a few steps from the door
with all the time in the world.

David Young

Elegy in the Form of an Invitation

James Wright, b. 1927, Martins Ferry, Ohio;
d. 1980, New York City

Early spring in Ohio. Lines
of thunderstorms, quiet flares
on the southern horizon.
A doctor stares at his hands.
His friend the schoolmaster
plays helplessly with a thread.

I know you have put your voice aside
and entered something else.

I like to think you could come back here now
like a man returning to his body
after a long dream of pain and terror.

It wouldn't all be easy:
sometimes the wind blows birds
right off their wires and branches,
chemical wastes smolder on weedy sidings,
codgers and crones still starve in shacks
in the hills above Portsmouth and Welfare . . .
hobo, cathouse, slagheap, old mines
that never exhaust their veins—
It is all the way you said.

But there is this fierce green
and bean shoots poking through potting soil
and in a month or so the bees
will move like sparks among the roses.

And I like to think
the things that hurt won't hurt you any more
and that you will come back
in the spring, for the quiet,
the dark shine of grackles,
raccoon tracks by the river,
the moon's ghost in the afternoon,
and the black earth behind the plowing.

In the Cities

Porphyro in Akron

I

Greeting the dawn,
A shift of rubber workers presses down
South Main.
With the stubbornness of muddy water
It dwindles at each cross-line
Until you feel the weight of many cars
North-bound, and East and West,
Absorbing and conveying weariness,—
Rumbling over the hills.

Akron, "high place",—
A bunch of smoke-ridden hills
Among rolling Ohio hills.

The dark-skinned Greeks grin at each other
In the streets and alleys.
The Greek grins and fights with the Swede,—
And the Fjords and the Aegean are remembered.

The plough, the sword,
The trowel,—and the monkey wrench!
O City, your axles need not the oil of song.
I will whisper words to myself
And put them in my pockets.
I will go and pitch quoits with old men
In the dust of a road.

II

And some of them "will be Americans,"
Using the latest ice-box and buying Fords;
And others—

I remember one Sunday noon,
Harry and I, "the gentlemen",—seated around
A table of raisin-jack and wine, our host
Setting down a glass and saying,—

      "One month,—I go back rich.
I ride black horse. . . . Have many sheep."
And his wife, like a mountain, coming in
With four tiny black-eyed girls around her
Twinkling like little Christmas trees.

And some Sunday fiddlers,
Roumanian business men,
Played ragtime and dances before the door,
And we overpaid them because we felt like it.

III

Pull down the hotel counterpane
And hitch yourself up to your book.

"Full on this casement shone the wintry moon,
And threw warm gules on Madeline's fair breast,
As down she knelt for heaven's grace and boon . . ."

"Connais tu le pays . . . ?"

Your mother sang that in a stuffy parlour
One summer day in a little town
Where you had started to grow.
And you were outside as soon as you
Could get away from the company
To find the only rose on the bush
In the front yard . . . .

But look up, Porphyro,—your toes
Are ridiculously tapping
The spindles at the foot of the bed.

The stars are drowned in a slow rain,
And a hash of noises is slung up from the street.
You ought, really, to try to sleep,
Even though, in this town, poetry's a
Bedroom occupation.

John Knoepfle

Church of Rose of Lima, Cincinnati

It looks from the hill like something
Fra Angelico painted, the red
rectangular lines and the bricked bell
steepled out of time. This church
honors Saint Rose in a city
as spare of Peruvians as miracles.

It floods out whenever the river rises
and has a smell of common water
at the altars, and pilots of tows
on long hauls from Pennsylvania
needle the dark with searching lights
to catch the hour off her clock.

Saint Rose keeps a timid time.
I've heard her bell strike three
as if an afternoon surprised her.
The church itself may well surprise her.
In Lima she has golden altars; Germans
made them wood on the unliturgical river.

But churches anywhere seem rude for her.
This virgin kept a hidden time
and the world could give no wedding ring
to wed her with. Her lover came quick
and killed the Peruvian roses she grew fond of
and the small buds withered in the winter fog.

Once I thought the rococo Christ
had made her a violent dove and held
her trembling in his hand like a bell.
I am not so sure of this today.
She may be undiscoverable, like silt
slow rivers encourage into islands.

Immigrant Children at Union School

We come from Bratislava and Wroclaw,
Budapest and Prague, Minsk and Tulcea:
a small United Nations in my kinder-
garten class. Our halting English
frustrates the teacher but never ourselves—
we know what we're trying to say.
We color and draw and listen
to a story read aloud about a missing
princess and the poor peasant boy
who must find her. All the girls
want to be the princess, all the boys
want to be the peasant. I just want
to be here in America, in Ohio,
in Cleveland, living on Salem Avenue
four houses from my grandparents,
and walking to Union School every
morning holding my grandfather's
right hand. I hardly want
anything else. But maybe three things:
to be smart enough to read English,
and brave enough to scold that princess
for getting lost, and kind enough not
to make fun of the girl from Hungary
with the bright red ribbon in her hair
who always draws her cats with eight legs.

Paul Zimmer

One for the Ladies at the Troy Laundry
Who Cooled Themselves for Zimmer

The ladies at the Troy Laundry pressed
And pressed in the warm fog of their labor.
They cooled themselves at the windows,
Steam rising from their gibbous skins
As I dawdled home from school.
In warmer weather they wore no blouses
And if I fought the crumbling coke pile
To the top, they laughed and waved
At me, billowy from their irons.

Oh man, the ladies at the Troy Laundry
Smelled like cod fish out of water,
And yet the very fur within their armpits
Made me rise wondering and small.

The Eisenhower Years

Flunked out and laid-off,
Zimmer works for his father
At Zimmer's Shoes for Women.
The feet of old woman awaken
From dreams, they groan and rub
Their hacked-up corns together.
At last they stand and walk in agony
Downtown to Zimmer's fitting stool
Where he talks to the feet,
Reassures and fits them with
Blissful ties in medium heels.

Home from work he checks the mail
For greetings from his draft board.
After supper he listens to Brubeck,
Lays out with a tumbler of Thunderbird,
Cigarettes and *From Here to Eternity*.

That evening he goes out to the bars,
Drinks three pitchers of Stroh's,
Ends up in the wee hours leaning
On a lamp post, his tie loosened,
Fedora pushed back on his head,
A Chesterfield stuck to his lips.

All of complacent America
Spreads around him in the night,
Nothing is moving in this void,
Only the feet of old women,
Twitching and shuffling in pain.

Zimmer sighs and takes a drag,
Exhales through his nostrils.
He knows nothing and feels little.
He has never been anywhere
And fears where he is going.

May I Ask You a Question, Mr. Youngstown
Sheet & Tube?

Mean grimy houses, shades drawn
Against the yellow-brown smoke
That blows in
Every minute of every day. And
Every minute of every night. To bake a cake or have a baby,
With the taste of tar in your mouth. To wash clothes
    or fix supper,
With the taste of tar in your mouth. Ah, but the grand
      funerals . . .
Rain hitting down
On the shiny hearses. "And it's a fine man he was, such a comfort
To his old ma.—Struck cold in the flower of his youth."
    Bedrooms
Gray—dim with the rumor of old sweat and urine. Pot roasts
And boiled spuds; *Ranch Romances* and The Bleeding Heart
Of Our Dear Lord—"Be a good lad . . . run down to Tim's
And get this wee pail filled for your old father now." The kids
Come on like the green leaves in the spring, but I'm not spry
Anymore and the missus do lose the bloom from her soft cheek.
(And of a Saturday night then, in Tim O'Sullivan's
    Elite Tavern itself:
"It is a world of sadness we live in, Micky boy."
"Aye, that it is. And better we drink to that."
"This one more, for home is where I should be now."
"Aye, but where's the home for the soul of a man!"
"It's a frail woman ye act like, my Micky."
"And it be a dumb goose who hasn't a tear to shed this night.")

Rain dripping down from a rusty eavespout
Into the gray-fat cinders of the millyard . . .
The dayshift goes on in four minutes.

❧ *Daniel Bourne*

Secrest Arboretum,
My Tenth Year in Wooster

(March 28, 1998)

Siberian larch, Tamarack, Norway
Spruce, Boxwood, Bourne. Yes,
I too am a transplant, the journey

to Ohio, the tongue
of the root system tangling
as it learns a new word for soil.

The vowels between the skinny leaves
and pliant needles. The consonants
like slight grooves in the bark.

Who knows the stories these trees
could have had? The Siberian Larch,
its fate sunk down in Ohio

in 1915, just escaping the Russian Revolution,
the silent parade of men beneath its branches
with guns pointed at the backs

of other men. The Norway Spruce
forming the great backbone of a house
destroyed by saturation bombing. The Boxwood's

deeply concentrated grain
hard to chop down, though its branches
will gladly sacrifice themselves

to the topiarist's delight.
The Tamarack brooding on the edge
of a cranberry bog.—And Bourne?

One ancestor came in 1838 to Ohio
to build a canal, but left soon after
to farm in Illinois. And his great-

great-grandson comes in 1988
to settle here, ten years later,
on the first green grass of late March

to look up in the branches
of another type of family,
its arms opened in welcome,

in blessing.

🖚 *Rachel Langille*

Mary Oliver Would

know what it's like
to wake up under
the sidelong glance
of buckeyes—
the garden already planted,
and nothing
remaining flat.

When I opened my eyes
on those Ohio hills,
the machined edges of Michigan
had vanished; I lay looking
into a subtle flow of water,
from the tilted bank
of a spring-fed pond—

no Adam about,
nailing a label on every
enigma: the view was mine,
the particulars
all ripplingly unnamed.
I had heard it dismissed—
*Ohio's dull, an empty puddle
on the Midwest map—*

yet here were peepers
brimming just beyond me,
conjuring a curl of
ferns from the damp earth,
lifting dreams
from their
rust-locked tombs.

Walking the children
to school those mornings,
I'd give myself to
earthworms glinting at the borders
of the sidewalk, clover
breezing up out of the cracks, while
God and the devil hummed medleys,
improvising in the ivy.

Among the shadows
and silence of my slow way
home, I touched
the thick-leaved rhododendrons—
taking all suggestions tucked inside
the folded purple arrowtips
of their moist buds.

Desire rose
from light in the last azaleas,
tracing curved brick archways
and the silken breastfeathers
of birds. Each time
I climbed the limestone path in Akron,
I wedded the fresh, the hidden
in Ohio earth.

Daniel Johnson

In a Steelworker's Bed

I once made love to a Polish woman
who was muscled like a horse and laughed
at my supple, whiskerless chin.

She shed her gravy-stained apron
where her husband hunkered
face down each morning

in work clothes with aching feet.
Semi trucks rumbled by on the overpass.
Sooty snow fell on the A-frame's roof.

I lay my head on the steelworker's
soft pillow. Listening for heavy footsteps.
Watching headlights sweep across the wall.

The steelworker's wife never turned
her sweat-beaded face from mine. Her chest
heaved like a bellows. Orange flames

licked the darkening Ohio sky.

ॐ Michael Salinger

cicadas

so thick
they were snow shoveled
from the sidewalks on public square
my grandfather called them canadian soldiers
but the thumb-sized black and green bugs
hadn't flown across lake erie
they clawed up from the soil
after seventeen year sleep
claim staking the world
for ten summer days
filling the stagnant air with static
then they died
leaving
empty shells
translucent chrysalis
split along the back
clinging to trees
and brick wall
their bodies
crunching under foot
and bus tire
downtown in front of higbee's
a doorman in a red coat
yellow trim at the cuffs
polished shoes
clears the entry
scrape of steel on concrete
white swath cutting through
the buzz-clicking mass
as if shaving a living beard
years ago
back when

playing with
mercury
on the black-and-white-checkered
asbestos-tiled kitchen floor
was not yet
dangerous

Rust Belt

After a year here we learn
they have a name, *Beaters*—
the ones without insurance
who don't give a shit,
who drive out-of-control
toboggans and just hope they slide
into one of those Jap cars with their huge
rusted Chevys, Fords, Pontiacs
with the big names, eaten so bad
they're just frames.
He gets welfare for cigarettes
and lotto, limps through the grocery
buying dented cans and no-name stuff,
leaves mufflers and tail pipes
in the road, curses me in my car
he didn't make, didn't pour
into a mold then piece together
because some hotshot thought small
cars were a fad, no fins.
He snorts at the poetry reading
in the paper, *Poems. That's what*
we're making now,
and after the reading, while
we're out looking at the Amish drive
their black sleighs, he keys a Subaru, slips
skating across the parking lot in old shoes,
and cheap wine drips from the bag
like a lung. If we were there we couldn't help
laughing, and he wouldn't even mind
because he knows people like us,
the ones who think they'll somehow get to the future
before he does.

Advent

Kids have sprayed the boulder
orange, given it
black eyes, a stitched
mouth. My neighbor tells
about the ferry, how birds
at the edge of Erie, whirling
in the white skies like pepper,
wait for blue weather, play
statues with a winter
that can open one gray eye
and freeze them halfway
across. We hang suet,
sow millet, as if winter
were another crop, snow warm
as cotton, sleet nourishing
as rice we would die without.
The leggy marigolds we pulled up
lie on the driveway
still pushing out their suns,
and we begin piling leaves,
stuffing them in plastic
sacks, stacking
the pillows so high
it must seem to the circling
birds, to the squirrels in their
holes, to the knuckleheaded
jack-o'-lantern in the park,
that we are hoping someone
will fall and save us.

Between Pittsburgh and Cleveland

What you notice first when you move
here is houses boarded like bandaged heads,
the ice-bound ships of empty steel mills,
old people sliding,
rusted cars spinning,
through slush
that packs and blackens behind wheels,
drops and lies in the road
like dead stars.

Next Sunday the Steelers play the Browns
but no one will watch—
we don't give one hundred and ten percent,
we don't take one game at a time.
We put on our pants one leg at a time,
and we sit on the bed to do it.
We're not going to rally
or regain the momentum.

Our sport is getting through the day,
the way in Scotland they run in only
jogging shoes up "fells," then back down
on paths of stones like bowling balls.

They say, we know this hill
can break bones.
We want to see if it will.

🌿 *Argie Manolis*

My Father's Secret

He was washing dishes
at Anthe's Restaurant in Akron
when they came after him
the first time. This isn't a secret.
He likes to tell how he tried to get out
of the back seat when the car had a flat.
The cop's hand on his neck.
The gun's barrel pressed to his temple.

Cold shower in prison,
dirty tin cup he threw at the wall,
the interpreter who warned him
he shouldn't cause trouble.

Don't ask for the rest of the story.
Let him skip to the church wedding
on the fourth of July.
Skip seven years to the first child,
two more years to the second.
Skip his wife's cancer, the funeral.

Then trace that path of words
back to their birthplace,
blackboard lessons for immigrants,
the yellow chalk spelling out
every necessary conjugation:
I eat, you eat, he, she, or it eats,

or back even further, to 1962,
the immersion, long jump
from the ship to Baltimore's shore.
No one to sing the baptismal hymn,
welcome him home.

Skip the mysterious journey
from Maryland to Michigan, or how
he found Theo Georgo in Detroit,
the first cousin he'd never met,
who gave him hot meals,
showers, a place to lay his head.

Tonight, he will almost say it:
She didn't love me at first.
But the long version is always
the better one: how they married
at first in court
so he could stay in the country,
"We wait over a year
before she decide
she want to get married for real
in church. The first time, we go out of state
so her name wouldn't be in the papers.
You know about this?"

And, of course, I will lie, ask him
to tell it again.

Dorothy Barresi

Nine of Clubs, Cleveland, Ohio

Thursday night: Progressive
Friday and Saturday nights: Eurostyle

Now I know there are bored, beautiful people everywhere.
The boys on their long stems of bones
waft and mingle, sipping Campari,

saying next to nothing to the girls.
Ecstasy is draining.
So is awe, anger, dread, tenderness

when frustrated by convention—any number of emotions
we will not see here tonight,
though we stand equidistant from dancefloor

and Lake Erie, gone back to solution this March
the way a bruise leaves a body.
All night ice loosens and grinds toward Canada.

We feel it more than hear,
and ore boats steer darkly
into the issuance of their lights, their names, as we did

not one hour ago, supplicants in the doorway's
jittery neon. We paid eight dollars to enter
what is spare, cool, clean.

We left behind fish stink and diesel fuel.
But what Europe is this?
Like the music, the dancers' faces

would give no clues. They are whiter than pain
or distraction; their arms dovetail as though
beneath black turtlenecks

a cavity waited, red and humming, for larval wings
to fold twice, re-enter.
I think this is the end of immigration.

I think if a live pig were thrown
skating and shitting onto the gorgeous dancefloor,
no one would stop posing, or crouch down

knife between his teeth
and stroking the smooth parquet croon
hunger, hunger, hunger

in his blood's first language.
The suburbs have given back their angels.
Refineries rise then sink like wedding cakes

into the filthy river—we've seen it often enough—
and it is wrongheaded or lachrymose
to wish the Old World back as well,

with its babushkas and lamentations, prayer cloths,
boats reeking of garlic cloves
by which we washed up on these shores. And the scythe

whistling at its uppermost arc—
"Di Provenza il mar, il suol."
The shining field,

the ugly babies in the architecture
puffing their thousand-year cheeks at us: I think
it wasn't ours, the past, and now

will never be, who left for better footing,
this purchase on brighter, quicker ground.
No tourist is ever innocent.

Tonight the music churns from hip to hip. The strobe light
won't make up its mind, but flickering hi-speed
erases half of all we see.

It's almost fun, this dancing.
And after, if the foreheads of the warehouses loom down
like character actors whose names

we're forever forgetting, say Ma Joad
or the Little Rascal's truant officer, that's okay.
We're lucky. Our car is right where we left it.

We're tired, sure. A little drunk.
The windshield weeps in a circle of streetlamp light and fog,
but we can drive all night if we want,

lose the lake lolling between these buildings
like a coated tongue,
head south to Akron or Columbus, or Xenia,

anywhere people routinely rise
from the absence of themselves, and begin the day new.
As we will here tonight in the tiny

bathroom crowded with our tribe and generation
bowing to mirrors,
the glimpse of smoky, downturned faces—
you, me, in ritual greeting to our neatly razored lines.

Henry Jacquez

A Dock Poem

for BJ

Here's your dock poem
Fork truck poem
Clattering teeth
Propane tank poem

A jackstacker poem
With face guard
Head shield
Steers in the opposite direction poem

Something blue collar
In southwest Ohio
Sleeves rolled up
A female unloading a semi poem

Write me something
Industrially skid & pallet
Heavy duty wheel chocks
And steel dock plates
Safety mirrors
Hydraulic stabilizers
Telescoping arm docklights
And forceful heaters

Something that meets OSHA requirements
With supportive supervisors
And an occasional Sunday
Of double time

Something involving loading
And unloading
Of eighteen wheelers
In the freezing snow

December Wake, Youngstown

In an ignorance of blossoms,
they are purple shivers and slate quasars—
no less beautiful for lack of a name.

Draped like holly over the casket,
they have been staged at each end like the terra cotta lambs
and shepherds of a Christmas crèche—there to witness

not the birth miracle, but the other one.
Sleeping among the retired steelworkers and ex-cops,
the teachers and his old union rep,

he has his glasses stationed to suggest a halftime Sunday nap
as though the Browns could rouse him when they emerge from the locker
    room
to the cheers of the second half; as though his eyes were a spark

away and the hands, now engaged, would slip their rosaries
for the remote control and a cold one, and even now,
we would simply agree to forget this whole thing and go on as before.

Cleveland, Angels, Ogres, Trolls

> *Drumcliff and Rosses are choke-full of ghosts. By bog, road, rath,*
> *hillside, sea border, they gather in all shapes: headless women, men*
> *in armor, shadow hares, fire-tongued hounds, whistling seals*
> *and others. A whistling seal sank a ship the other day.*
> —*Yeats*, The Celtic Twilight

Still today, sober and tenured as I can be,
I go back. When I close my eyes it's Cleveland,
I've fallen out of puberty, lost the beast's
rough hair and heavy hurt. Angels go with me.
To be means giving credence without question.
The mirror's a miracle even before I take off
my clothes. Aunts work wonders
with their crazy praying. Novenas shatter glasses
poised in palsied hands of drunks, the lame
leap and whirl like windy leaves. Kennedy
comes back, Jackie at his side unbloodied,
his skull smooth and whole as the schoolroom globe.
Old men stop by to sharpen scissors or haggle
for the family's rags, their carts powered by song.
We pray for the conversion of Russia.
The whole world's Catholic, it rains new babies
every night, nothing in the world's to be
discounted and hordes of children meet each day
to learn to do and say, eyes glowing streetlamp bright
with currents of perfect fear, all joy.
Nothing tastes the same. Ogres and trolls
patrol the dark beneath each bed. Where I step
glaciers have been and may come again.
Tomorrow the sun will rise forever.

David Brendan Hopes

East Akron

1

White spring beauty
and pink spring beauty,
the white violet.

The Canadas trumpet over Alder Pond,
neither settling nor soaring,
ecstatic and inconsolable,

in one last winter cry.

2

We were wrong in our youth
when we said we would make poetry.
The song makes the singer,
nor is there any song
without the throat and heart unmade,
and hence wrought new as on an anvil,
unrecognizable to itself.

3

So for half an evening I took the geese to task
for their hysterical lament.
Settle for the night, or brave deep heaven and be done.
So I walked to the brim of the cold lake
and cried to them, enough!
Then the ones that had been crying
and the ones that had been silent
rose, all rose and made their orbits
between the lake and sky, neither tightening
nor letting loose, circling and crying,
a cyclone feathering the water backward

from the downstroke of its wings,
and I realized they were answering me,
that my voice through the forest had become the song
it would fall forever short of singing:
a thunder of April on the troubled water,
inconsolable, ecstatic,
my lion's head to theirs thrown back at sunset,
roaring.

I had cried in goose, desire.

Beating with black wings ceaseless
under the first four stars.

Paul Christensen

Strolling over the Rhine in Cincinnati

One more heartbreak bar on a corner
and the neighborhood is
moored forever to this world.

A church closed up and moved
to the suburbs, to be nearer the believers.
The heathens stayed put in their

dark drapes, with the storm door
double bolted against chaos.
A wire forest of antennas reaches

into the obscure sky for news
and consolation, like underwater
tentacles siphoning for food.

The idle stare from bus stops,
park benches; a blind opens
between dirty fingers for a glimpse.

Responsibility begins in dreams,
idle fantasies spent over coffee
and a boiling egg, wandering

where America has drifted to,
with so much cut away from
the heart, so little to embrace.

Lament for My Brother

Many nights these days he's out beneath the stars,
a bottle of single malt in a brown bag
that wrinkles in his hand like a shrunken head,
walking with his friend, Ken, and a girl from work,
all from night shift. Tonight they've all worked
doubles, they're wired, the air electric in their lungs.
Ross takes a swig, wipes the lip with his sleeve,
and hands the bottle off to light a cigarette,
exhaling the storm cloud upward into night.
He thinks he sees his whole future in the smoke.
What'll you have? he says to smoky figures,
wiping out the inside of a rinsed-off shot glass.

Ken jangles the keys and says, My place.
The three walk in. They light a joint
and lie back on the bed, still gazing at stars.
My brother nestles his thigh against the girl's.
All three pass the limp ashen knuckle
from their fingers to their lips. O night!
tonight spare them the day's demands,
let them be unaware of death, that other
sleep, and grant them every wish. Let them
breathe in the crisp night air you were perhaps
saving for autumn, and let them be here forever,
where lakes have thawed and walleye swim again.

Sarah Gail Johnson

Love Songs for Cleveland

I

We hang on to the rail
as Cleveland dies
into morning,
our sweet breath pushing through
the skyline's metal lungs.
The roar of a fist hitting glass.
Time to go home,
the bouncer says, *Jesus,*
you desperate people—
we love you but go home.

II

Down the bloodshot coast,
strippers count their money.
Sugar crusts the maple trees,
blanketing our coffee table.
Children dream of beaches
dark as God's blue eye.
After years of rooms
intimate as parking lots,
how can we lay our heads
in beds of untouched snow?

III

At the church wedding in Chardon,
the bride cries into her cigarettes.
Whites suck themselves from clouds.
Under her dress, the garter flashes
unavoidable as death.
The best man whispers to the preacher:
rock and roll is dead.

IV

I find him lost on Cedar Avenue,
his head between his knees.
We are broke as the river
in the polluted sludge of March,
unnaturally fast and green.

Snow on our noses.
Down at the Flats, we dismember
the strung-out stars, giving
each constellation a child's name.

V

Under the cold amphitheater of streetlights,
we walk to our apartment that reeks
of rented lives, late night diner omelets
of electricians and nurses.
A promise: tomorrow
we'll do this again, but better.
Sweet wind from Lake Erie
undoes my hair with curses.

In the next room, two medical students touch
each other, gutting the sick walls
of our house. After their hands
have known the terror of cadavers,
where do they go?

VI

Cleveland, I thought you were dirty.
I thought you were already dead.
But I have looked everywhere
for this hard mystery:
rust, steam, bricks, and sweat,
old bridges groaning
over water, the river on fire
like a dead woman's wig.

Buildings still as punished
children leaning in.
Eyes bright like the mirrored rack of gin,
show me how to prove my love.
Send me to the stadium
late in winter,
the Indians already lost,
without a ticket or a daughter.

Philip Levine

One for the Rose

Three weeks ago I went back
to the same street corner where
27 years before I took a bus for Akron,
Ohio, but now there was only a blank space
with a few concrete building blocks
scattered among the beer cans
and broken bottles and a view of
the blank backside of an abandoned hotel.
I wondered if Akron was still down there
hidden hundreds of miles south among
the small, shoddy trees of Ohio,
a town so ripe with the smell
of defeat that its citizens lied
about their age, their height, sex,
income, and previous condition
of anything. I spent all of a Saturday
there, disguised in a cashmere suit
stolen from a man twenty pounds
heavier than I, and I never unbuttoned
the jacket. I remember someone
married someone, but only the bride's
father and mother went out
on the linoleum dance floor and leaned
into each other like whipped school kids.
I drank whatever I could find and made
my solitary way back to the terminal
and dozed among the drunks and widows
toward dawn and the first thing north.
What was I doing in Akron, Ohio
waiting for a bus that groaned slowly
between the sickened farms of 1951

and finally entered the smeared air
of hell on US 24 where the Rouge plant
destroys the horizon? I could have been
in Paris at the foot of Gertrude Stein,
I could have been drifting among
the reeds of a clear stream
like the little Moses, to be found
by a princess and named after a conglomerate
or a Jewish hero. Instead I was born
in the wrong year and in the wrong place,
and I made my way so slowly and badly
that I remember every single turn,
and each one smells like an overblown rose,
yellow, American, beautiful, and true.

Beyond Even This

Beyond Even This

Who would have thought the afterlife would
look so much like Ohio? A small town place,
thickly settled among deciduous trees.
I lived for what seemed a very short time.
Several things did not work out.
Casually almost, I became another one
of the departed, but I had never imagined
the tunnel of hot wind that pulls
the newly dead into the dry Midwest
and plants us like corn. I am
not alone, but I am restless.
There is such sorrow in these geese
flying over, trying to find a place to land
in the miles and miles of parking lots
that once were soft wetlands. They seem
as puzzled as I am about where to be.
Often they glide, in what I guess is
a consultation with each other,
getting their bearings, as I do when
I stare out my window and count up
what I see. It's not much really:
one buckeye tree, three white frame houses,
one evergreen, five piles of yellow leaves.
This is not enough for any heaven I had
dreamed, but I am taking the long view.
There must be a backcountry of the beyond,
beyond even this and farther out,
past the dark smoky city on the shore
of Lake Erie, through the landlocked passages
to the Great Sweetwater Seas.

The Buckeye

We learned about the state tree
in school—its fruit
so useless, so ugly

no one bothered to
commend the smudged trunk
nor the slim leaves shifting

over our heads. Yet
they were a good thing to kick
along gutters

on the way home,
though they stank like
a drunk's piss in the roads

where cars had smashed
them. And in autumn
when the spiny helmets split

open,
there was the bald
seed with its wheat-

colored eye.
We loved
the modest countenance beneath

that leathery cap.
We, too, did not want to leave
our mothers.

We piled them up
for ammunition.
We lay down

with them
among the bruised leaves
so that we could

rise, shining.

Ruth L. Schwartz

Ohio Highway

As if I'd failed to love, and needed
to be shown again:

the birds falling like darkened snow
to the fertile ground,

the birds flocking like lovers' hands
to the damp of green.

Green of the highway median,
narrow planted strip of life—

while on the heated current
rising from the road,

three red-tailed hawks angle their black
bodies through the sky,

their hunger certain,
hovering, transparent—

and all of us humans in cars on the highway,
maybe eighty miles an hour,

braiding our way through painted lanes
in a kind of dance,

sometimes the semis honking
to keep the beat,

and at the overpass—it's raining now—
two longhaired teenage girls on the bridge

waving to the steady passing
of the cars—and I think they think they love us

like an ocean, like we love anything
larger than us,

which goes on in spite of us,
utterly apart from us:

the rain like longing made visible,
filtered through the sieve of sky;

the birds which, any way they fly,
are always flying home.

Jeff Mann

German Village

for Cindy and John

History has followed us here
across a galaxy of cold gray water.
Within the maples' October smolder,
staked heretics shriek in the town square,
books blacken along Unter den Linden,
the chimneys of Buchenwald sigh
their sooty breath. Even in heaven
we cannot forget conflagrations,
gathering up the bouquets of burning,
maple leaves we press to our faces,
breathing deep their fire.

This is the afterlife we want: a universe
of brick, extensions of every earthly
appetite, recompense for every suffered
sorrow. An immigrant dreams of density:
slate-roofed cottages, chimney pots,
embroidered lintels, limestone stoops.

And chrysanthemum dusk, a cold wind
curling our collars up. The saved
soon learn how simply blessing's bred:
brisk walks along brick streets and autumn air,
church spires spiked with moonlight.
Night harvests the brittle wings of bats,
rakes and rustles leaf-scattered streets.
Outside the brew-pub's golden windows,
the darkness sharpens, waits and yearns.

Now our names are called, we enter in.
Angels appear with steins of lager,
platters of sauerkraut and wurst,
Kartoffelsalat mit Speck, cherry strudel
furbelowed with whipped cream and folksong.
Beneath the table you squeeze my thigh.

Tonight we will lie together beneath quilts,
warm and naked, watching hearth-fire dwindle.
Long after midnight I will wake, close the flue,
curl against you, listening to heaven's dark breath,
hard wind shaking flame from maple boughs.

❧ *David Ray*

Ohio

The script never changes, though the actors are replaced.
—R. D. Laing

Born after a snowy night, so white—
my daughter—to a mother from Ohio
who once drove alone, straight to Chicago
where I first saw her on the sidewalk
putting coins into a traffic meter,
then later came across her in a bar—
where she warned right at the outset
that she was the hysterical-seductive type,
whatever that meant—I had to find out—
and thus in due time I fathered her child,
born in a snowstorm when, waking at dawn
with her labor approaching, I trudged up the hill
to recover my car—that battered green Volks
with its hood bashed in by a deer.
The fact of it is I had forgotten the car,
left it parked overnight outside my office.
I made my way uphill through snow, slipping on ice.
My glasses froze with frost and big flakes.
Cold helped to wake me, though not enough
for enlightenment. It should have been
a wiser man who greeted his newborn daughter
about 7 that morning. Had her mother stayed
in Ohio and had we not shared a few beers,
we would never have had our daughter,
nor would mother and child have returned
to Ohio, nor later would that daughter, too,
with her daughter repeat the same journey.
To the young I'd advise not to wed shotgun
when a mean Dean of Students, irate that you two
are rumored by her spies to be shacked up

near campus, gives you three days to prove
you are married—which we did with a quick trip
to a J.P. in Angola, famed for its brutal prison.
With so many mothers with infants in their arms
fleeing home to Ohio, it's no wonder Madonna
and child are the subject of paintings, although
no artist yet has depicted Grandmother
and Grandfather young and drunk, just starting out.

Godspeed

During his first orbit, I lay
in a hospital bed, wrapped
in a piano concerto by Brahms
which someone had turned on
by accident, my black-haired son
bundled in his isolette, caught up
in the first of wordless dreams
he would never learn to compromise,
while an Ohio-born traveler
circled our adventure with his own.

When we met him years later,
stumping Ohio in the seventies,
he crinkled his eyes and said
I looked like Annie. She told me
they eat by candlelight every night,
even if it was only hot dogs.

Last week my son, late bloomer,
weightless with euphoria, married
the girl he said he had to have,
and today the old astronaut,
launched safely again into space,
comments on the beauty of Hawaii,
where perhaps the honeymooners
find a moment to shield their eyes
and scan the sky.

On my refrigerator a clipping—
Annie brave in a pale hat,
her balding husband's hand

on her shoulder, reminder
that all adventurers who soar
must then descend, survive
the terrors of re-entry, and find
their footing on this common ground.

for John and Annie Glen
and John and Sara Spidel
October, 1998

Finvola Drury

Now, Children, Let Us All Rise
and Sing the State Song

But first let me tell you about the snapdragons
the pink ruby yellow and white ones
in the tall footed glass my grandmother
used for celery
it's on the old secretary
we shouldn't have cut down
so that it could no longer hold
The World's Hundred Greatest Detective Stories
in their bright red bindings
I got through all of one vacation
sitting in the brown velvet chair with the ottoman
my aunt gave my uncle for his birthday
in Bay Village
right on the lake outside of Cleveland
just down the road
from where that summer a man told the police
a bushy-haired intruder
had gotten into the house and murdered
his wife
and they searched and searched for a person
fitting that description
but they never found one and my uncle
was sure they never would
because the man had killed his wife himself
but the jury would not
recommend the death penalty he said
later during the trial
because they would deliver the verdict
on Christmas Eve
and no jury ever did that to a man
on Christmas

his father whose photograph
stood on the table next to the velvet chair
had witnessed an execution once
in some official capacity
and afterward had thrown up
he was a rock-ribbed Republican
my aunt said
so I wondered a lot about that
because
somebody was always
getting the chair in Ohio
and if it happened as it usually did
at night
my mother would sit on the couch
across from the radio
near the wall where she had put
a picture
of Mary Magdalene bared to the waist
and kneeling
with her long hair hanging down
and when time ran out and the Governor's call
didn't come
she'd always say
some poor mother's heart is broken tonight
hers was anyway
it got to be part of our evening programs
after Jack Armstrong and The Lone Ranger
and Little Orphan Annie
we stayed tuned in for the execution
we knew by heart what would happen
the condemned man ate a hearty dinner
the priest administered the last rites
there was the long walk to the green door
and then
the strapping in
Columbus

was the Capitol of punishment
and as all those men went so my brother might
come under a bad influence
and end up like Jimmy Cagney instead of Pat O'Brien
in the movies every Saturday
because we were poor and Irish
and hadn't she seen him
behind the window of the pool hall on Main Street
chalking up a cue tip
as cool as a cucumber a cigarette
dangling from between his lips
and he was there with her in the stands
the night
the Mangan girls and I
and hundreds of others
danced under the lights
in the huge stadium
and the Governor rode around and around waving
his hat
from the back seat of an open car
while the band played Beautiful Ohio
and my mother had told me earlier
fixing my hair in the bedroom
she hated him
the tree surgeon
and we stood in a ring and waved back
in our pink ruby yellow and white
dresses.

⚬ Linda Frost

The Buckeye Sestina

*Who would have thought the afterlife would
look so much like Ohio?*
        —Maggie Anderson

*Then I went down
to a black creek and alder grove
that is Ohio like nothing else is . . .*
        —Mary Oliver

Ohio like nothing else is, you say in your book
and go on about snowfall, alders, creeks, and state
birds. Your peers laud grain and mourn reservoirs
now dried up, and Maggie in Kent said heaven is Ohio,
or at least what comes after, which is just what I
feared. From the time I was ten, I wanted to leave.

And I did finally, at eighteen, finally leave
Mom's tears, Dad's shop, Field High. But earlier, in books,
I'd been leaving for years. I was bored and I
hated the flat hills and alfalfa fields of the state,
and when I went to college, I skipped Ohio,
scotched it, trashed it in the reservoir.

Only a year before, our friend by the reservoir
died in his car on prom night when he went to leave
the dance drunk. His Pinto flipped on its top, its Ohio
plates thrown thirty feet from the car. The yearbook
eulogized the driver, but didn't mention the state
in which they found him, choked on the bottom's mud. I

remember, too, how that summer we got stoned in Dave's drive, our eyes
red as robins, and there was no better place than Mogadore Reservoir
(down by the Anchor where the girls stripped to their barest states
every Thursday night) to walk the shore, kick the leaves,

and end up way too late in the back of his Barracuda, buried in books
and baring as much as you dared, for your first sex in Ohio.

Mary and Maggie, you can picnic where you like and write it up as Ohio.
For me, it'll always be six-packs at Annette's and parties where I
never got to kiss Jeff Matulis, though I was reassured by that book
that said men never love what's good for them. Love is a reservoir
of cheap grief. Memory is when your senses won't take their leave.
State of mind, of grace, of being; whether West Virginia or a state

we could stand, nothing could touch our Buckeye state.
Whatever else, it was ours, and for a have-little girl in Ohio,
that was something. But I didn't then love it, still wanted to leave
and see what artistic, fantastic, romantic world lay beyond what I
could find at home. My imagination swelled, a fat reservoir
of deep dreams, and I set out to find—it's no surprise—my best life in books.

A small town place, Maggie calls it in her book, and she's right, I know,
but in its wholly flatness, Ohio returns to me now as a singular state,
one I still can't leave, not any more, not with the reservoir waters wailing.

Ohio Haiku

1

Why did those pioneers, having come this far, decide
To stop? They must have known, by scout
Or second sight, that nothing lay ahead but Indiana.

2

Under this sudden embarrassment of snow, the last leaves lie
Plastered like a bald man's nightmare:
Little wet toupees stuck crooked on the skull.

3

The quaint pavements of Paris, the flagstone squares of Florence
Have their charm in tourist photographs, but we've got
The real slideshow here: the streets of Akron cobbled in ice.

4

I'm no scholar of politics, no minister of history,
But I believe what that good book said:
All the presidents nobody ever heard of came from Ohio.

5

That squirrel at the bird feeder, that pirate of seeds,
Why isn't he scrabbling on the lawn,
A buccaneer of buckeyes and the lesser nuts?

6

Driving to Athens from the east, you must first go through
Guysville and Coolville, as if Plato's *Republic*
Were printed inside a comic book, in the hairy panels of R. Crumb.

7

If you know what the weeping cherry weeps for, and why
The willow hangs its head in the wind,
Then how can you tap this maple for its sticky tears?

8

—Lake at the top end, river at the bottom, and both holding back
Those low fields, that flat middle the hills keep
Slipping down to, as if land, like water, seeks its own level.

9

Custer, that boy-general, native son of this state,
Sweetened his locks with oil of cinnamon.
Three days after he fell, you could still smell him on the dead slope.

10

Not okra, but corn; not crawfish, but pike;
No Fat Tuesday, but a full
Year of seven thin days to the week.

11

If Adam had been dusted off in Ohio, he and Eve would
Own a small orchard somewhere near Seville,
Selling, from their roadside stand, jugs of cider with a homely bite.

12

In this city too new for temples, too busy
To dig up a buried word or bone,
I lean on my own past, the only ruin still standing.

John Chapman

He wore a tin pot for a hat, in which
he cooked his supper
toward evening
in the Ohio forests. He wore
a sackcloth shirt and walked
barefoot on feet crooked as roots. And everywhere he went
the apple trees sprang up behind him lovely
as young girls.

No Indian or settler or wild beast
ever harmed him, and he for his part honored
everything, all God's creatures! thought little,
on a rainy night,
of sharing the shelter of a hollow log touching
flesh with any creatures there: snakes,
raccoon possibly, or some great slab of bear.

Mrs. Price, late of Richland County,
at whose parents' house he sometimes lingered,
recalled: he spoke
only once of women and his gray eyes
brittled into ice. "Some
are deceivers," he whispered, and she felt
the pain of it, remembered it
into her old age.

Well, the trees he planted or gave away
prospered, and he became
the good legend, you do
what you can if you can; whatever

the secret, and the pain,

there's a decision: to die,
or to live, to go on
caring about something. In spring, in Ohio,
in the forests that are left you can still find
sign of him: patches
of cold white fire.

Tecumseh

I went down not long ago
to the Mad River, under the willows
I knelt and drank from that crumpled flow, call it
what madness you will, there's a sickness
worse than the risk of death and that's
forgetting what we should never forget.
Tecumseh lived here.
The wounds of the past
are ignored, but hang on
like the litter that snags among the yellow branches,
newspapers and plastic bags, after the rains.

Where are the Shawnee now?
Do you know? Or would you have to
write to Washington, and even then,
whatever they said,
would you believe it? Sometimes

I would like to paint my body red and go out into
the glittering snow
to die.

His name meant Shooting Star.
From Mad River country north to the border
he gathered the tribes
and armed them one more time. He vowed
to keep Ohio and it took him
over twenty years to fail.

After the bloody and final fighting, at Thames,
it was over, except

his body could not be found.
It was never found,
and you can do whatever you want with that, say

his people came in the black leaves of the night
and hauled him to a secret grave, or that
he turned into a little boy again, and leaped
into a birch canoe and went
rowing home down the rivers. Anyway,
this much I'm sure of: if we ever meet him, we'll know it,
he will still be
so angry.

Ohio

We were excited at the motel
when the B. B. King tour bus
pulled in but then my mother said
"where did all these colored come from?"
She's eighty-five.
That's how it is in Ohio.

No it's not, that's how it is
in us, that's why 35 years ago
in my first year at Cornell
we elected the one black kid in my class
president though no one talked to him
and that's why last year when someone
left the note "DIE NIGGER" on Denise's desk
everybody said they couldn't *imagine* what
cretin would do a thing like that.

And I think that's why the great dream
of middle-class whites is to lie face down
on a chaise by a pool in the sun,
left alone, not moving; why they dream
of a state as close to death as possible,
flat, bland, unending, like the Ohio
Turnpike and all the motels off it
and the food shops with their vats of grease
and their smells of burning fats and chemical
donuts glazed orange and blue and green
and the embalmed meats in infinite variety.
And no one murmurs: they buy and eat and eat.

David Shevin

Three Miles from Luckey

I was speeding past the meanclean suburban streets
bound south for Seneca County route twenty
on a night of pitch and tar sky—no moon,
stars spun at far reach of this galaxy
cold and big; I was watching the deep dark
closing hug of the roads. Sign said I was
three miles from Luckey. Felt like it.
Echoes whispered secrets on the distant air's hush.

Time was the lone critter we could not turn upside
down in those days. It pushed behind movement
back there in the city, where some poor devil
might find half a sandwich uneaten, or a silent
porch where a sleeping family might not notice
so that he might rest for an hour himself. Couldn't
win for losing, cuz luck was rose iron and my hands
filled with lead. Lord, if I'd had to carry a wooden

cross that would be lightweight compared to the time
on my hands. So I don't know—honest—what all
the hurry was. Mexican camps breathed life past
night's hedgerows. A mariachi was singing his child
his own story. I hadn't worked since the paint plant
ran out my sick time, and there wasn't no point
to return where an hour on the job I'd be fainting
again. When the unstable spirit comes around to anoint

all our chances in luck and in love, well, he must
be blind drunk is all I can figure. There used to be
a family on the Old Fostoria Road, father did investigation
part time, and I heard that the mother—a ditzy
woman with kids from another marriage, long gone—

would sometimes drive the new child, a restless son
named Arthur, up the road to Bethel Baptist in Fostoria
just so that he'd hear the good gospel sound in his one

crack at toddlerhood. Maybe he was born to the wrong culture
or the right one for him. I don't know. Me, I was raised
for the college my daddy wanted but I never did, and I mention
Arthur cuz up in Toledo, there he was on the way to praise
his professor, gunna make it in psych, he tells me. And maybe
I'm not sure what the hungry was all about. Had a good bet
to be back to let the dog out, to be off that road in that time
before sleep came nagging. And maybe all the hope we can get

is imagining something like skyscrapers of the beloved community
on northwest Ohio's flat horizon, a country in need
of an active volcano, in need of more kindness, in need
of tapping the wealth of those hearts that reflexively feed
their own through the seasons of snowstorms and hails.
Dim light blurred out the south side, and I slowed.
I'd once hit a startled bird, and remembered like a shock
that you never know what small lives might appear on the road

that feels like it's all of your darkness, all your own.
I was still three miles from Luckey, and on my way home.

🙊 *James Reiss*

The Breathers

(Jeffrey Andrew Reiss—October 5, 1969)

In Ohio, where these things happen,
we had been loving all winter.
By June you looked down and saw your belly
was soft as fresh bread.

In Florida, standing on the bathroom
scales, you were convinced—
and looked both ways for a full minute before crossing
Brickell Boulevard.

In Colorado you waited-out summer in a mountain
cabin, with Dr. Spock,
your stamps, and my poems in the faint
8000-foot air.

> Listen, he had a perfect body,
> right down to his testicles, which I counted.
> The morning he dropped from your womb, all rosy
> as an apple in season, breathing the thick
> fall air of Ohio, we thought good things would happen.

> Believe me, Dr. Salter and the nurses were right:
> he was small but feisty—they said he was
> *feisty.* That afternoon in his respirator
> when he urinated it was something to be proud of.
> Cyanotic by evening, he looked like a dark rose.

Late that night you hear . . .

> Think of the only possible twentieth-century consolations:
> Doris saying it might have been better this way;

think of brain damage, car crashes, dead soldiers.
Better seventeen hours than eighteen, twenty years
of half-life in Ohio where nothing happens.

Late that night you hear them
in the . . .

For, after all, we are young, traveling
at full speed into the bull's eye of the atom.
There's a Pepsi and hot dog stand in that bull's eye,
and babies of the future dancing around us.
Listen, the air is thick with our cries!

Late that night you hear them
in the nursery, the breathers.
Their tiny lungs go in and out like the air
bladder on an oxygen tank
or the rhythm of sex.
Asleep, your arms shoot towards that target
with a stretch that lifts you like a zombie,
wakes you to the deafening breathers.

And now you see them crawling
rings around your bed, in blankets,
buntings, preemies in incubators circling
on casters, a few with cleft palates, heart trouble,
all feistily breathing, crawling
away from your rigidly outstretched arms—
breathing, robbing the air.

Sharon Kourous

How We Argue

I

We come from slow flat places in Ohio,
places bumbling beside a river
or rising at a crossroads
after miles of corn.
The skies are flat.
Our arguments are quiet.
Tight lips, silence,
an angry shoulder at the kitchen sink,
stillness of wheat,
wind in a cornfield;
the stubborn small town
grassblade-in-the-teeth quiet
of Ada, Cary, Sandusky, Findlay;
the rivers: Ottawa, Maumee, Blanchard, Tiffin
shouldering through hot baked clay
to sullen Erie.

II

Men remember nitro in the wagons,
nestled like eggs
in rustling straw;
they hunched over reins,
patient, careful, eyes out for rocks,
ruts, roadholes.
Knowing anger
a risky luxury,
they blasted roadways,
stumps of trees;
drained the swampland
down to shallow Erie.
In front of post offices, on benches,

they quarrel silently
with their
recalcitrant land.

III
My mother clenched clothespins
with her teeth,
hanging out the wash; moved
to the next task
stiff-shouldered;
out of cracked gray clay,
insisted on
the reluctant beans, peas, berries:
mouthing around the wooden pins
her arguments with God.

IV
The Maumee moves
through a stubborn land;
argues with limestone, tree stumps, bridges;
in a quarrel with gravity,
slips with muddy refusal
into cloudy Erie.
The lights go on in small towns
along Ohio's rivers:
the gas station lights,
the stop light,
the tavern's red wink;
and out among the cornfields
the old two-window, wide-front-porch
brick farmhouses
fist their lights
across the stubborn fields.

v

When we shout,
something really big is required:
God, a tornado,
the Depression. Our angers
tend to ruminate on porches
or lie wakeful
in the square of moonlight
on the blanket;
quiet anyway,
like the kicked dog
still running in his sleep
on the shadowed sill.

Stanley Plumly

Buckeye

My father came to Ohio
the year the war ended.

There were four of us, pinched in with possessions,
in a '29 Ford sedan.

You had to wind it up
and even then it farted
& spat back.
Five times it wanted to break my bony arm.

Mother sat in the backseat with my sister.
My father drove like a soldier
home from the front.
I was six and crazy
to be killed.

We drove all that first day until after dark,
Ohio being north of the way things were.

Contributors

🐝 *Maggie Anderson's* fourth collection is *Windfall: New and Selected Poems,* from the Pitt Poetry Series. She has received awards from the National Endowment for the Arts, the Ohio Arts Council, the Pennsylvania Council on the Arts, and the MacDowell Colony. She teaches creative writing at Kent State University, where she directs the Wick Poetry Program and edits the Wick Poetry Series published by the Kent State University Press.

🐝 *Ron Antonucci,* former editor of *Ohio Writer,* sits on the board of the Poets and Writers League of Greater Cleveland and is a member of the Poetry Council at Cleveland State University. His poems, reviews, articles, and essays have appeared in a wide variety of magazines and newspapers, including the *Cleveland Plain Dealer, The Akron Beacon Journal, Pudding Magazine, Penthouse Publications, Isaac Asimov's Science Fiction Magazine, Kirkus Reviews,* and *Library Journal.* He is assistant director at the Hudson Library and Historical Society.

🐝 *David Baker* is the author of eight books, most recently *Changeable Thunder* (University of Arkansas Press, 2002) and *Heresy and the Ideal: On Contemporary Poetry* (Arkansas, 2000). Among his awards are fellowships and prizes from the Guggenheim Foundation, the National Endowment for the Arts, the Ohio Arts Council, the Society of Midland Authors, and the Poetry Society of America. Baker moved to Ohio in 1984 and currently resides in Granville, where he serves as poetry editor of *The Kenyon Review.* He teaches at Denison University and in the MFA program for writers at Warren Wilson College.

🐝 *Ivars Balkits,* from Appalachian Ohio, works as adult program coordinator for the Athens Public Library. A 1999 recipient of an Ohio Arts Council's Individual Artist Fellowship, he has been published in *Sonoma Mandala, Grasslands Review, New York Quarterly, The Prose Poem (2x),* and in two anthologies: *A Measured Response* and *Smashing Icons.* Two poems have been selected for an upcoming anthology, *Appalachia Uncovered.* Balkits is working on an historical play about coal mining and labor history in the Hocking Valley coalfields of Ohio.

🐝 *Dorothy Barresi,* a former resident of Akron, is the author of *All of the Above* (Beacon Press, 1991) and *The Post-Rapture Diner* (University of Pittsburg Press, 1996), which won an American Book Award. Her poems have appeared in *The Harvard Review, Parnassus, The Kenyon Review,* and *Poetry.* Her essay-reviews of contemporary poetry appear regularly in *The Gettysburg Review.* She directs the creative writing program at California State University—Northridge, where she is a professor of English.

◈ *Elinor Benedict*, a native of Tennessee and graduate of Duke University, earned an MA in English from Wright State University, Ohio, and an MFA in Writing from Vermont College. Her poetry collection, *All That Divides Us*, won the 2000 May Swenson Poetry Award (Utah State University Press). She is founding editor of *Passages North* literary magazine. She lived in Ohio from 1956–77 and from 1981–95, but now divides her time between the Upper Peninsula of Michigan and Florida.

◈ *James Bertolino's* book *Making Space For Our Living* (Copper Canyon Press, 1975) was reprinted online in 1999 by CAPA: Connecticut College's Contemporary American Poetry Archive. His *26 Poems from Snail River* (Egress Studio Press) was published in 2000, as was his chapbook *Greatest Hits: 1965–2000* (Pudding House Publications). He has poems in recent anthologies from HarperSanFrancisco, Milkweed Editions, University of Utah Press, New Rivers Press, Kodansha International, and Helicon Nine Editions. His magazine publications include *Ploughshares, The Montserrat Review, Notre Dame Review, Beloit Poetry Journal* and such online publications as *Switched-on Gutenberg, Mudlark, Salt River Review,* and *Clean Sheets*. Bertolino was a visiting professor at Willamette University in Oregon for 1998–99 and has since returned to the creative writing faculty at Western Washington University.

◈ *Eric Birkholz*, a native of Youngstown, works as a professional editor in Washington, D.C. His poems have appeared in *Antietam Review, Barrow Street, Coe Review,* and *Painted Bride Quarterly,* and he was recently awarded a fellowship from the Virginia Commission for the Arts. He received his MFA from the University of Arizona and lives with his wife and daughter in Arlington, Virginia.

◈ *Terry Blackhawk* graduated from Antioch College in the 1960s. She lives and writes in Detroit, Michigan, where she directs InsideOut, a writers-in-schools program she founded for Detroit youth in 1995. She is the author of *Body & Field* (Michigan State University Press, 1999) and a chapbook, *Trio: Voices from the Myths* (Ridgeway Press, 1998).

◈ *Robert Bly* is the author of the bestseller *Iron John,* which launched the men's movement to national fame, as well as ten collections of poetry, most recently *Morning Poems* (HarperPerennial, 1998) and *Eating The Honey of Words: New and Selected Poems* (HarperFlamingo, 1999). He lives in Minneapolis, Minnesota.

꙾ *Imogene Bolls*, professor emerita of English and former poet-in-residence at Wittenberg University, has retired to Taos, New Mexico, to continue to write. Author of three volumes of poetry, including *Advice For The Climb* (Bottom Dog, 1999) and more than six hundred poems published in journals and anthologies, she is the recipient of two Ohio Arts Council grants and the 1995 Ohioana Poetry Award.

꙾ *Daniel Bourne's* first book, *The Household Gods*, was published by the Cleveland State University Poetry Series in 1995. His poems have also appeared in *Field, American Poetry Review, Ploughshares, Shenandoah, Chariton Review, Poetry Northwest, Salmagundi, Mid-American Review,* and *Indiana Review.* The recipient of several Ohio Arts Council poetry fellowships, he teaches at the College of Wooster, where he edits *Artful Dodge.* In 1985–87, he was in Poland on a Fulbright for work on the translation of younger Polish poets and has since returned four times. His translations of Tomasz Jastrun have appeared in several magazines and in his full-length collection *On the Crossroads of Asia and Europe* (Salmon Run Press, 1999).

꙾ *Steve Brightman*, born in 1967, received a BA from Mount Union College and an MA from Eastern Kentucky University.

꙾ *Sue D. Burton* is a physician assistant at a women's health center in Vermont. Her poetry has appeared in *Calyx, Harvard Review,* and *Onion River: Six Vermont Poets.*

꙾ *Hale Chatfield* (1936–2000), a native of Passaic, New Jersey, was founder and editor of *Hiram Poetry Review.* Professor Emeritus of English at Hiram College, he was awarded fellowships from the National Endowment for the Arts and the Ohio Arts Council, and received the Poetry Award from the Ohioana Library Association. In his career, he published eighteen books, most of them poetry.

꙾ *Paul Christensen* has two new books of poems, *Hard Country* (Thorpe Springs, 2001) and *Blue Alleys* (Martin House, 2001). He was a National Endowment for the Arts poetry fellow in 1991 and received a Distinguished Prose Award from *Antioch Review* and a Best Fiction Award from the Texas Institute of Letters. His new memoir, *West of the American Dream: An Encounter with Texas,* was issued by Texas A&M Press in 2000. His edition of nineteenth-century American protest poetry will be published by Oxford University Press.

꙾ *David Citino*, a native of Cleveland, is professor of English and creative writing at The Ohio State University. His new book of poems is *The Invention of Secrecy* (The Ohio State University Press, 2000). He writes on poetry for the *Columbus Dispatch* and is the contributing editor of a book of prose, *The Eye of the Poet,* from Oxford University Press.

ஜ *Jeanne E. Clark's* collection *Ohio Blue Tips* won the 1998 Akron Poetry Prize and was published by The University of Akron Press in 1999. She is an assistant professor of creative writing at California State University, Chico.

ஜ *Hart Crane* (1899–1933), one of the most respected and influential of the second generation of Modernist poets, was born in Garrettsville, Ohio, and grew up in Warren and Cleveland. In 1926, he published his classic first book of poems, *White Buildings,* and followed that, in 1933, with *The Bridge,* his long poem about American experience.

ஜ *Mary Crow,* Poet Laureate of Colorado, grew up in Loudonville, Ohio, and did her undergraduate work at the College of Wooster. She is the author of nine books—four volumes of poetry and five of translation of Latin American poetry. Her most recent book of poems is *I Have Tasted the Apple* (BOA, 1996). She teaches in the creative writing program of Colorado State University.

ஜ *Christine Delea,* raised in Long Island, New York, lived in Ohio from 1978 to 1983. She received her BA from Marietta College, her MA from Marshall University, and her PhD in English from the University of North Dakota. She now lives in Oregon with her husband, Mel White. She has twice been nominated for Pushcart Prizes and has won an Academy of American Poets Award. Her chapbook, *Ordinary Days in Ordinary Places,* was published by Pudding House (2000). Most recently, her poems have appeared in *Rattapallax, Heliotrope, Phoebe: Journal of Feminist Scholarship, Theory, and Aesthetics, Concho River Review, Pinyon Poetry,* and *A Gathering of the Tribes.*

ஜ *Ron Domen,* born and raised in Ohio, graduated from Warren Western Reserve High School and from Youngstown State University. His poems have appeared in *Riverwind, Grasslands Review, Whiskey Island Magazine, Slipstream,* and *Yarrow.* He is a physician and associate professor at The Milton S. Hershey Medical Center and The Penn State University College of Medicine, Hershey, Pennsylvania, where he also teaches in the Department of Humanities.

ஜ *Rita Dove,* born and raised in Akron, is Commonwealth Professor of English at the University of Virginia. From 1993 to 1995, she served as Poet Laureate of the United States. Among her many honors and awards are Fulbright, Guggenheim, and Mellon fellowships and the NAACP Great American Artist Award. She has published six books of poetry, including the 1987 Pulitzer Prize–winner *Thomas and Beulah* and *On the Bus with Rosa Parks* (Norton, 1999).

ஜ *Finvola Drury,* born in Cleveland, received her BA from State University of New York, Empire State College, and her MA from State University of New York at Buffalo. She has published two books, *Elegy for Joric Ross* and *Burning the*

Snow, and her magazine appearances include *Poetry*, *60's Without Apology* (University of Minnesota), *Conservatory of American Letters Anthology*, *New Rivers Irish American Anthology*, *Aurora Anthology* (Bull Thistle Press), and *A Broadside for Broadside* (University of Illinois at Chicago). She received the First Annual Writing in Rochester Award for Teaching of Writing, 1994.

Thomas Dukes is professor of English at The University of Akron where he teaches business and professional writing, modern British and American literature, and gay studies. His poems have appeared in *Poetry*, *The Jabberwock Review*, and other journals. He lives in Richfield, Ohio.

Linda Nemec Foster is the author of five collections of poetry; the most recent, *Amber Necklace From Gdansk*, was published by Louisiana State University Press in 2001. Her poems have appeared in *The Georgia Review*, *Nimrod*, *Quarterly West*, *DoubleTake*, *Mid-American Review*, and *River Styx*. She has received awards from the National Writers' Voice Project, the Arts Foundation of Michigan, and the Michigan Council for the Arts. Her work has also been cited in the *Pushcart Prize Anthology*. Born in Cleveland, Ohio, Foster currently resides in Michigan.

Robert Fox, a native of Brooklyn, New York, settled permanently in Ohio after moving to Athens in 1967. He has been publishing poems in literary magazines since 1963. His *Greatest Hits, 1965–2000* was published by Pudding House (2000). His short fiction has won PEN Syndicated Fiction and Nelson Algren awards, and December Press has published two collections. He has been literature program coordinator of the Ohio Arts Council since 1977.

Linda Frost, born at Akron General Hospital and raised in Suffield, Ohio, is now an associate professor of English at the University of Alabama at Birmingham. Her poems have appeared in such journals as *Columbia*, *Rhino*, *Sing Heavenly Muse!*, and *Witness*, and she is the editor in chief of *PMS*, a journal of women's poems, memoirs, and short stories.

David Lee Garrison teaches Spanish and Portuguese at Wright State University. His poetry, criticism, and translations have appeared in journals such as *Colorado Review*, *The Literary Review*, and *The Nation*. He has published two books of poems: *Blue Oboe* (Wyndham Hall Press, 1984) and *Inside the Sound of Rain* (The Vincent Brothers Review, 1997).

Elton Glaser, a native of New Orleans, has lived in Ohio since 1972. Distinguished Professor Emeritus of English, he edits the Akron Series in Poetry for The University of Akron Press. He has published four full-length collections of poetry, most recently *Winter Amnesties* (Southern Illinois University Press,

2000). Among his awards are two National Endowment for the Arts fellowships, four fellowships from the Ohio Arts Council, and the 1996 Ohioana Poetry Award. His poems have appeared in the 1995, 1997, and 2000 editions of *The Best American Poetry*.

෨ *Alvin Greenberg* is a poet, fiction writer, essayist, and librettist. His latest collections of poetry include *Why We Live with Animals* (Coffee House Press, 1990), and *Heavy Wings* (Ohio Review Press, 1988). His most recent collection of short stories, *How the Dead Live,* appeared in 1998 from Graywolf Press. He has also collaborated on three operas with composer Eric Stokes, most recently *Apollonia's Circus* (premiered at the University of Minnesota, 1994), and his personal essays have been appearing in *The Georgia Review, Antioch Review, American Literary Review,* and elsewhere. After teaching for thirty-four years in the Macalester College English Department in St. Paul, Minnesota, he has moved to Idaho where his wife, poet Janet Holmes, has taken a position in the MFA program at Boise State University.

෨ *William Greenway,* a native of Georgia, has taught for the past fifteen years at Youngstown State University, where he is professor of English. He won the 1997 Larry Levis Editors' Prize from *Missouri Review,* the 1993 Open Voice Poetry Award from The Writer's Voice, the 1993 State Street Press Chapbook Competition, the 2001 Ohioana Poetry Award, and was 1994 Georgia Author of the Year. His fourth full-length collection of poems, *Simmer Dim,* was published by The University of Akron Press in 1999.

෨ *Jeff Gundy* has taught English and writing at Bluffton College in northwest Ohio since 1984. His books include *Inquiries, Flatlands,* and *Rhapsody with Dark Matter* (poems), and *A Community of Memory: My Days with George and Clara* (creative nonfiction). He has received four Ohio Arts Council grants and two C. Henry Smith Peace Lectureships. His work has appeared in *Georgia Review, Shenandoah, Mid-American Review, Beloit Poetry Journal,* and many other magazines.

෨ *Richard Hague* was born and raised in Steubenville, Ohio. His degrees in English are from Xavier University in Cincinnati, and he has taught writing, interdisciplinary studies, and literature at Purcell Marian High School in Cincinnati since 1969. His books of poems include *Ripening* (Ohio State University Press, 1984), *Possible Debris* (Cleveland State University Poetry Center, 1988), and *A Bestiary* and *Greatest Hits: 1968–2000,* both from Pudding House. *Milltown Natural: Essays and Stories from A Life* (Bottom Dog Press, 1997) was nominated for a National Book Award.

Gwen Hart grew up in Painesville, Ohio. She has earned degrees from Wellesley College and Hollins University and is looking forward to entering an MFA program with her husband, Roger, a fiction writer. The Harts currently live and write on the Outer Banks of North Carolina.

 Rick Hilles, born in Canton, Ohio, received a BA/LSM from Kent State University and an MFA from Columbia University. His poems have appeared recently in *Poetry*, *The Nation*, *The New Republic*, and *The Paris Review*. Among his awards and honors are fellowships from the Wallace Stegner Program at Stanford University and the Institute for Creative Writing at the University of Wisconsin at Madison, and the Larry Levis Editors' Prize from *The Missouri Review*. He teaches English and creative writing at the University of Wisconsin in Madison.

 Marianna Hofer has published poems, stories, and book reviews in a number of magazines. She teaches English at the University of Findlay and has had a residency at the Ragdale Foundation.

 David Brendan Hopes is professor of literature and language at the University of North Carolina at Asheville, founder and editor of Urthona Press, and founder and director of the Black Swan Theater Company. He is the author of the Juniper Prize and Saxifrage Prize book, *The Glacier's Daughters* (University of Massachusetts Press, 1981), and of *Blood Rose* (Urthona Press, 1997), *A Childhood in the Milky Way* (The University of Akron Press, 1999), and *A Sense of the Morning* (Milkweed Editions, 1999). His work has appeared in periodicals such as *The New Yorker*, *Audubon*, *Christopher Street*, and *The Sun*.

 Kathleen Iddings's sixth book of poetry, *Sticks, Friction and Fire: Selected and New Poems*, was published by West Anglia Publications in 2001. Recipient of a National Endowment for the Arts Fellowship, among other honors and awards for poetry, she has published more than four hundred poems. Iddings is editor and publisher of San Diego Poet's Press and La Jolla Poet's Press.

 Bonnie Jacobson lives in Beachwood, Ohio. She is the author of two poetry collections, *Stopping for Time* (GreenTower Press, 1989) and *In Joanna's House* (Cleveland State University Press Poetry Press, 1998). Her poems have most recently appeared in *The Iowa Review*, *The Gettysburg Review*, and *Tar River Poetry*. In 1999, the Ohio Arts Council awarded her an Individual Artist Fellowship.

 Henry Jacquez is the president of the Greater Cincinnati Writer's League. He has an Associate of Arts degree from the University of Cincinnati and works for the General Electric Company. His poems have been published in *Common Threads*, *Wind Chimes*, and *Free Lunch*, among other periodicals and anthologies.

৯৫ *Daniel Johnson* grew up in Salem, Ohio. He now lives in Chicago and works as an arts coordinator at the Association House of Chicago. He is an MFA student at Warren Wilson College.

৯৫ *Sarah Gail Johnson,* a native of Minneapolis, is currently a James A. Michener Fellow in Austin, Texas. In addition to poetry, she writes essays and fiction. Her work has appeared in several journals and anthologies, most recently *The Madison Review.*

৯৫ *Diane Kendig* was born, raised, and educated in Ohio. She is the author of literary translations, fiction, essays, a children's musical, and poetry, including two chapbooks of poetry, most recently *Diane Kendig's Greatest Hits 1978–2000* (Pudding House). The recipient of two Ohio Arts Council Individual Artist Fellowships in poetry and a Yaddo fellowship, she teaches at the University of Findlay and has devoted much of her extracurricular time to creative writing workshops in public schools and prisons in the United States and Nicaragua.

৯৫ *Judy Klare* has published two chapbooks, *Fountains in Common Places* and *Searching for Universal Verbs* (Writer's Works Chapbooks, 1999), and two books for teens, *Self-Esteem* and *Manners* (Rourke Publishing Group, 1989, 1990). A teacher/psychologist, she has spent much of her career at Ohio University in Athens.

৯৫ *John Knoepfle* grew up in Cincinnati, Ohio, and graduated from Xavier University after World War II. In the 1950s, he tape-recorded the recollections of Ohio River tow and packet steamboat men. The tapes and transcripts of these interviews are housed in the Public Library of Cincinnati and Hamilton County. In 1986, he received the Mark Twain Award for Distinguished Contributions to Midwestern Literature at Michigan State University. He is the author of seventeen books of poetry, including *Poems from the Sangamon* (University of Illinois Press, 1985) and *Begging an Amnesty* (Druid Press, 1994). A new collection of poems, *Prayer against Famine and Other Irish Poems,* will be published in 2002.

৯৫ *Sharon Kourous,* born in Oregon, Ohio, currently lives in nearby Rossford. She earned her BE and MA degrees from the University of Toledo and teaches high school English. A Pushcart nominee, she has published poetry in such journals as *The Atlanta Review, The Formalist,* and *The Lyric.* Recently, she has preferred the speed and intimacy of the Internet, appearing in *The Melic Review, Poet's Canvas,* and many other electronic zines.

৯৫ *Rachel Langille* teaches creative writing, literature, and composition courses at Mott Community College in Flint, Michigan. Her poems have appeared in *English Journal, Louisiana Literature, The MacGuffin, The Peralta Press,* and *The*

Wallace Stevens Journal, among others. She lived in Ohio from August 1983 through September 1986, earning an MA in English from The University of Akron.

❧ *Cathy Lentes* lives with her husband and three children in an 1890s farm-house in southeast Ohio a few miles from the Ohio River. Her writing about Appalachian Ohio appears in a variety of journals and magazines. Her poem, "Approaching Chester, Ohio," won the 2000 Appalachian Poetry Award from East Tennessee State University and *Now & Then* magazine.

❧ *Philip Levine* is the author of sixteen books of poetry, most recently *The Mercy* (Knopf, 1998). His other poetry collections include *The Simple Truth* (Knopf, 1994), which won the Pulitzer Prize; *What Work Is* (Knopf, 1991), which won the National Book Award; *Ashes: Poems New and Old* (Atheneum, 1979), which received the National Book Critics Circle Award and the first American Book Award for Poetry; *7 Years From Somewhere* (Atheneum, 1979), which won the National Book Critics Circle Award; and *The Names of the Lost* (Windhover Press, 1976), which won the Lenore Marshall Poetry Prize. He has received the Ruth Lilly Poetry Prize, the Harriet Monroe Memorial Prize from *Poetry,* the Frank O'Hara Prize, and two Guggenheim Foundation fellowships. For two years, he served as chair of the literature panel of the National Endowment for the Arts, and he was elected a chancellor of The Academy of American Poets in 2000. Philip Levine lives in New York City and Fresno, California, and teaches at New York University.

❧ *Anthony Libby* wrote his first poem at the age of forty-five; since then, his poetry has been published in such journals as *The Alaska Quarterly Review, The Antioch Review, The Santa Barbara Review,* and *The Southern Review.* He teaches in the English Department at Ohio State University and is the author of numerous critical articles on modern poetry and painting, as well as the critical book *Mythologies of Nothing: Mystical Death in American Poetry* (University of Illinois, 1984). *The Secret Turning of the Earth* was a winner of the Wick Poetry Chapbook Competition at Kent State University.

❧ *Joanne Lowery*'s poems have appeared in many literary magazines, including *Spoon River Poetry Review, Laurel Review, Birmingham Poetry Review,* and *River Styx.* She was born in Cleveland, Ohio, and grew up in suburban Parma. Currently, she lives in Michigan.

❧ *Jeff Mann* grew up in southwest Virginia and southern West Virginia, receiving degrees in English and forestry from West Virginia University. He has published in *Kestrel, The Laurel Review, Antietam Review, Poet Lore, The Hampden-Sydney Poetry Review, Journal of Appalachian Studies, Spoon River Poetry Review,*

Callaloo, and *Prairie Schooner.* His collection of poems *Bliss* won the 1997 Stonewall Chapbook Competition and was published in 1998 by BrickHouse Books. *Mountain Fireflies,* which won the 1999 Poetry Matrix Chapbook Series, and *Flint Shards from Sussex,* which won the Gival Press Chapbook Competition, were published in 2000. He teaches Appalachian studies and creative writing at Virginia Tech.

ᘍ *Argie Manolis,* a native of Akron, Ohio, and a graduate of Kent State University, teaches creative writing and composition at the University of Minnesota, Morris. She has an MFA in poetry from Arizona State University. Her poems have appeared in *Spoon River Poetry Review* and *Nimrod,* among other magazines.

ᘍ *William Matthews* (1942–97), one of America's finest and most influential contemporary poets, was born in Cincinnati. He was the author of several volumes of poetry, most recently *After All: Last Poems* (Houghton Mifflin, 1992), and won the National Book Critics Circle Award for *Time and Money* (Houghton Mifflin, 1995), in 1995, and, in 1997, the Ruth Lilly Award from the Modern Poetry Association. He was professor of English and director of the writing program at City College of the City University of New York.

ᘍ *Ron McFarland* was born in Bellaire, Ohio, and attended school through second grade in Barnesville, after which his family moved to Florida. He presently teaches seventeenth-century and modern poetry, Hemingway seminars, and contemporary Northwest writers courses at the University of Idaho, where he was named the first state writer-in-residence in 1984. In 1985–86, he was an exchange professor at Ohio University, and he visits his parents periodically in rural Belmont County. His book of new and selected poems, *Stranger in Town,* was published in 2000 by Confluence Press.

ᘍ *Glenn McKee,* born in Hartville, Ohio, earned degrees from Earlham College (BA, 1955) and Tufts University (MST, 1961). Retired in Maine after a varied career in the Protestant ministry, journalism, and human services administration, Glenn has now lived in New England for over forty-five years. McKee's Ohio poems comprise the bulk of his 1999 collection, *Memory's Menu,* from Mellen Poetry Press.

ᘍ *Ray McNiece* is the author of three books of poems, *Dis* (Burning Press), *The Bone-Orchard Conga* (Poetry Alive Publications), and *The Road that Carried Me Here* (Bottom Dog Press, 1998). He has authored two solo theater works and numerous poetry/music collaborations with Tongue in Groove. He has performed with Lawrence Ferlinghetti, with Robert Bly, and with Yevgeny Yevtushenko at the Moscow Polytech.

𝕒 *Ann E. Michael* lives in Pennsylvania, where she has been a fellowship recipient in poetry from the Pennsylvania Council on the Arts. She is an essayist, newspaper columnist, radio commentator, and arts educator. Her work has appeared in *Poem, Natural Bridge, Coe Review,* and other literary journals, as well as in numerous anthologies.

𝕒 *John N. Miller* has had four articles on Nathaniel Hawthorne published in scholarly journals. He has also published poems in a wide variety of literary journals.

𝕒 *Robert Miltner* is assistant professor of English at Kent State University—Stark, where he teaches creative writing, composition, and literature. Miltner earned his PhD from Kent State University with a dissertation on Raymond Carver's poetry. He is the author of three poetry chapbooks: *On the Off-Ramp* (Implosion Press), *The Seamless Serial House* (Pudding House), and *Against the Simple* (Kent State University Press, 1995). Miltner's poems have appeared in *Birmingham Poetry Review, Wisconsin Review, Whiskey Island, The Vincent Brothers Review, The New York Quarterly, English Journal, Monserrat Review,* and *Barrow Street.*

𝕒 *Ed Ochester's* most recent books are *The Land of Cockaigne* (Story Line Press, 2001), *Cooking in Key West* (Adastra Press, 2000), and *Snow White Horses: Selected Poems 1973–1988* (Autumn House Press, 2000). Former director of the creative writing program at the University of Pittsburgh, he is the editor of the Pitt Poetry Series and teaches in the Bennington MFA Writing Seminars.

𝕒 *Mary Oliver,* an Ohio native, lives in Provincetown, Massachusetts, and teaches part of the year at Bennington College in Vermont. Among her most recent books are *The Leaf and the Cloud: A Poem* (DaCapo Press, 2000) and *Rules for the Dance: A Handbook for Writing and Reading Metrical Verse* (Houghton Mifflin, 1998). A much honored poet, Oliver has received for her work both the Pulitzer Prize and the National Book Award.

𝕒 *Kenneth Patchen* (1911–72), born in Niles, Ohio, authored over forty books of poetry, prose, and drama, and pioneered the poetry-jazz movement in America. He received the Shelley Memorial Award and the National Foundation on the Arts and Humanities Award.

𝕒 *Deanna Pickard* has won two Ohio Arts Council Fellowships and two Montgomery County Fellowships. She has published in *Poetry, Antioch Review, New England Review,* and *The New Republic.* Recent poems appear in *River Styx, Crazyhorse, The Vincent Brothers Review,* and *Poetry Northwest.*

❀ *Stanley Plumly*, a native of Barnesville, Ohio, was raised in rural Ohio and Virginia. Currently a professor of English at the University of Maryland, College Park, he has published eight books of poetry, most recently *Now That My Father Lies Down Beside Me: New & Selected Poems, 1970–2000* (Ecco Press, 2000).

❀ *Lynn Powell's* book *Old & New Testaments* (University of Wisconsin Press) won the 1995 Brittingham Prize in Poetry and the 1996 Great Lakes Colleges New Writers Award. A native of east Tennessee, Powell has lived in Oberlin, Ohio, since 1990.

❀ *Kevin Prufer* grew up in Cleveland. He is the author of *The Finger Bone* (Carnegie Mellon, 2001) and *Strange Wood* (Winthrop Poetry Series, 1998). He is the editor of *The New Young American Poets* (Southern Illinois University Press, 2000) and *Pleiades: A Journal of New Writing*. His poems are in *Ploughshares, Triquarterly, The Southern Review, The Antioch Review, Boulevard,* and elsewhere.

❀ *David Ray's* books of poetry include *Wool Highways* (Helicon Nine Editions, 1992; the William Carlos Williams Award from the Poetry Society of America) and *Kangaroo Paws: Poems Written in Australia* (Thomas Jefferson University Press, 1995). His latest publication is *Demons in the Diner,* which received the Richard Snyder Award from Ashland Poetry Press in 1999. David Ray lives in Tucson.

❀ *James Reiss,* the author of four books of poems, most recently *Ten Thousand Good Mornings* (Carnegie Mellon University Press, 2001), as well as the editor of *Self-Interviews: James Dickey* (Dell, 1972), is professor of English at Miami University in Oxford, Ohio, and editor of the Miami University Press.

❀ *Philip St. Clair,* born in Warren, Ohio, in 1944, is the author of four books of poetry, most recently *Acid Creek* (Bottom Dog, 1997). He has received fellowships from the National Endowment for the Arts and the Kentucky Arts Council. His poems have appeared in *Black Warrior Review, The Gettysburg Review, Harper's, Ploughshares, Poetry Review, Prairie Schooner, Shenandoah,* and elsewhere. He lives with his wife, Christina, in the Appalachian mountains of Carter County, Kentucky.

❀ *Michael Salinger* has been writing and performing poetry and fiction for over twenty years. His work has appeared in dozens of literary journals, including *Poetry, Sapphire Magazine, Taproot, Northern Ohio Live, Modern Machine Shop,* and the *Cleveland Free Times.* Five-time captain of the Cleveland Slam team that represented the city at the National Poetry Slam competition, he is the founder and director of the Nova Lizard Project, a performance troupe in Cleveland, Ohio. His latest publication, *Sunday Morning,* has recently been released by Burning Press. He lives in Mentor, Ohio.

Vicki Schwab, teacher and writer, lives in Columbus, Ohio. She teaches writing at Ohio Dominican College and at The Ohio State University and is seeking publication for her nonfiction manuscript "The Color of Ice".

Ruth L. Schwartz has received grants from the National Endowment for the Arts, the Ohio Arts Council, and the Astraea Foundation, as well as numerous literary prizes. Her first book of poems, *Accordion Breathing and Dancing*, won the 1994 Associated Writing Programs competition and was published by the University of Pittsburgh Press in 1996. She taught at Cleveland State University for two years and is currently on the creative writing faculty at California State University, Fresno.

Ellen Renée Seusy was born in Albuquerque, New Mexico, and received degrees from the University of New Mexico and Stanford University. She is currently working on her MFA at The Ohio State University in Columbus, where she has lived since 1986. Her work has appeared in *Century Magazine, Cottonwood*, and *The Briar Cliff Review.*

David Shevin moved to Ohio from New York in 1974. He teaches at Central State University, in Wilberforce, Ohio. His books of poetry include *The Discovery of Fire* (1988) and *Needles and Needs* (1994), both from Bottom Dog Press.

Larry Smith grew up in the industrial Ohio Valley. He teaches at Bowling Green State University's Firelands College in Huron, Ohio, and received the Ohioana Poetry Award for 1999. His *Thoreau's Lost Journal: Poem* was published in 2001 by Westron Press of Toledo.

Merry Speece lived most of her life in rural Ohio before moving to Columbia, South Carolina, in 1989. She has published two chapbooks of poetry and has been a recipient of a fellowship in prose from the South Carolina Arts Commission.

Lianne Spidel taught high school in Ohio for twenty-five years and now teaches creative writing at Edison College in Greenville. Her poems have appeared in *Hiram Poetry Review, Wisconsin Review, Grand Lake Review, Folio, Poetry*, and *Shenandoah*, among others. With Myrna Stone and David Lee Garrison, who appear in this volume, she is a member of the Greenville Poets.

Myrna Stone's poems have appeared in *Poetry, TriQuarterly, Ploughshares*, and *Green Mountains Review*, as well as many other journals. She is the recipient of two Ohio Arts Council Individual Artist Fellowships in Poetry and a Full Fellowship to Vermont Studio Center. Her first collection, *The Art of Loss*, was published by Michigan State University Press in 2001.

John Streamas is an assistant professor at Washington State University. He has won the Wise-Susman Prize of the American Studies Association and has published in critical journals and collections. In Syracuse's writing program in the 1980s, his advisors were George P. Elliott and Raymond Carver.

Ann Townsend's first collection of poetry, *Dime Store Erotics* (Silverfish Review Press), was published in 1998. Her poems, stories, and essays have appeared in such magazines as *The Nation, The Paris Review,* and *Poetry.* She teaches at Denison University in Granville, Ohio.

G. C. Waldrep has work in recent issues of *Poetry, Ascent, Many Mountains Moving,* and other journals. His book *Southern Workers and the Search for Community* is available from University of Illinois Press. As an Amishman with friends all over Indiana, he frequently travels through Ohio by bus.

BJ Ward was recently named Distinguished Teaching Artist by the New Jersey State Council on the Arts, and Teaching Artist of the Year by Playwrights Theatre of New Jersey for his work in the New Jersey Writers Project. His most recent volume of poetry, *17 Love Poems with No Despair* (North Atlantic Books), was chosen by Borders.com as one of the sixty-two Essential Books for the 1998 Dodge Poetry Festival. His first book, *Landing in New Jersey with Soft Hands,* also from North Atlantic, was published in 1994. His work has appeared in journals such as *Poetry, The Paterson Literary Review, Long Shot, The Black Swan Review, Kimera, Lips,* and *NEBO.* He is the recipient of poetry fellowships from the New Jersey State Council on the Arts and the Alliance for Arts Education in New Jersey. He teaches creative writing at Warren County Community College and directs the Warren County Poetry Festival, in New Jersey.

Julie Herrick White has an MFA from Warren Wilson College. Her publications include *Friends from the Other Side,* a poetry chapbook by State Street Press; *Steubenville,* a poem sequence by Pearl Editions; and *Uncle Gust and the Temple of Healing,* short fiction by the Indianapolis Writers' Center Press.

James Wright (1927–80) has made his hometown of Martins Ferry world famous. He is one of the most influential and admired poets of the last fifty years, and his *Collected Poems* won the Pulitzer Prize in 1971. Wright attended Kenyon College, served with the United States Army in Japan during the American occupation, and studied at the University of Washington under Theodore Roethke. He taught at a number of colleges, including Hunter College in New York City. The James Wright Poetry Festival is held annually in Martins Ferry, Ohio.

꧂ *David Young*, who has taught at Oberlin College for forty years, has published nine volumes of poetry, most recently *At the White Window* (The Ohio State University Press, 2000). His volume of selected poems, *The Planet on the Desk* (1991), was published by Wesleyan University Press. He is a founder of *Field* magazine and an editor with the Oberlin College Press, which publishes many poetry titles. His recognitions include a Guggenheim Fellowship, an Ohio Major Artist Award, and the Cleveland Arts Prize. He is also very active as a translator (German, Czech, Chinese, Italian).

꧂ *Paul Zimmer* has published eleven books of poetry, including *Family Reunion* (University of Pittsburgh Press, 1983), which won an Award for Literature from the Academy and Institute of Arts and Letters; *The Great Bird of Love* (University of Illinois Press, 1989), which was selected by William Stafford for the National Poetry Series; *Big Blue Train* (University of Arkansas Press, 1993); and *Crossing to Sunlight: Selected Poems* (University of Georgia Press, 1996). In recent years, his essays have been published in such magazines as *The Georgia Review, The Gettysburg Review, The Southern Review,* and *Ohio Review.* He has received two fellowships from the National Endowment for the Arts and three Pushcart Prizes. He was associate director of the University of Pittsburgh Press and director of the university presses at Georgia and Iowa. He currently lives on a farm in Wisconsin and spends part of each year in a small house in the south of France.

Credits

Maggie Anderson. "Beyond Even This," from *A Space Filled with Moving*, University of Pittsburgh Press, copyright © 1991 by Maggie Anderson. Reprinted by permission of the University of Pittsburgh Press.

Ron Antonucci. "Final Nature Poem on the Little Cuyahoga," copyright © 2000 by Ron Antonucci. Used by permission of the author.

David Baker. "Dixie," from *Sweet Home, Saturday Night*, University of Arkansas Press, copyright © 1991 by David Baker. Reprinted by permission of the author. "Midwest: Ode," from *Changeable Thunder*, University of Arkansas Press, copyright © 2001 by David Baker. Reprinted by permission of the University of Arkansas Press.

Ivars Balkits. "Regional Bird," copyright © 2002 by Ivars Balkits. Used by permission of the author.

Dorothy Barresi. "Nine of Clubs, Cleveland, Ohio," from *All of the Above*, Beacon Press, copyright © 1991 by Dorothy Barresi. Reprinted by permission of Beacon Press, Boston.

Elinor Benedict. "The Curse of Purslane," copyright © 2002 by Elinor Benedict. Used by permission of the author.

James Bertolino. "Home in Ohio," from *First Credo*, Quarterly Review of Literature Poetry Series, copyright © 1986 by James Bertolino. Reprinted by permission of the author.

Eric Birkholz. "December Wake, Youngstown," copyright © 2002 by Eric Birkholz. Used by permission of the author.

Terry Blackhawk. "Good Friday at the Rookery," first published in *Spoon River Poetry Review*, copyright © 2001 by Terry Blackhawk. Reprinted by permission of the author.

Robert Bly. "Driving through Ohio," from *Silence in the Snowy Fields*, Wesleyan University Press, copyright © 1962 by Robert Bly. Reprinted by permission of Wesleyan University Press and the author.

Imogene Bolls. "Crossing Mac-o-Chee Creek," copyright © 2002 by Imogene Bolls. Used by permission of the author.

Daniel Bourne. "Secrest Arboretum, My Tenth Year in Wooster," first published in *85 Acres on Route 83*, The Wooster Book Company, copyright © 1998 by Daniel Bourne. Reprinted by permission of the author.

Steve Brightman. "Benefits of Geauga County," copyright © 2002 by Steve Brightman. Used by permission of the author.

Sue D. Burton. "Brick," copyright © 2002 by Sue D. Burton. Used by permission of the author.

Index of Poets and Titles

About the Editors

Elton Glaser, Distinguished Professor of English Emeritus at the University of Akron and former director of The University of Akron Press, edits the Akron Series in Poetry. He has published four full-length collections of poems: *Relics, Tropical Depressions, Color Photographs of the Ruins,* and *Winter Amnesties.* His poems have appeared in the 1995, 1997, and 2000 editions of *The Best American Poetry.* Among his awards are two fellowships from the National Endowment for the Arts, four fellowships from the Ohio Arts Council, the Iowa Poetry Prize, and the 1996 Ohioana Poetry Award.

William Greenway, a native of Georgia with a BA from Georgia State University and a PhD from Tulane University, is a professor of English at Youngstown State University. He has published two chapbooks and four full-length collections of poetry, most recently *Simmer Dim* in the Akron Series in Poetry. He was named Georgia Author of the Year in 1994 and received the Ohioana Poetry Award in 2001.

About the Book

I Have My Own Song for It: Modern Poems of Ohio was designed and typeset by Kachergis Book Design of Pittsboro, North Carolina. The typeface, Monotype Dante, was designed by Giovanni Mardersteig who made his typographic reputation with the magnificent books he designed and printed on the hand press at his Officina Bodoni before the second World War.

   I Have My Own Song for It: Modern Poems of Ohio was printed on 50-pound Sebago Antique Cream by Hamilton Printing Company of Rensselaer, New York.